Documentary in a
Changing State
Ireland since the 1990s

Documentary in a Changing State

Ireland since the 1990s

EDITED BY

CAROL MacKEOGH &
DÍÓG O'CONNELL

CORK UNIVERSITY PRESS

First published in 2012 by
Cork University Press
Youngline Industrial Estate
Pouladuff Road, Togher
Cork, Ireland

British Library Cataloguing in Publication Data
A CIP catalogue record for this book is available from the British Library.

ISBN-978-1859-18491-2

Typeset by Tower Books, Ballincollig, Co. Cork
Printed by Gutenberg Press, Malta

www.corkuniversitypress.com

For Greer and Stevie

For Aoife, Ailíse and Clíona

In memory of Mary Raftery (1957–2012)

Contents

III Documentary: Policy and Politics

IV Towards the Future: Interviews with Key Players

Tables

List of Illustrations

Acknowledgements

The editors would like to acknowledge the contributions of all speakers, delegates and volunteers at the Documentary Conference in November 2007 at the Institute of Art, Design and Technology (IADT), Dún Laoghaire, out of which this book emerged. We would also like to thank all the contributors for their hard work and patience and for contributing their thoughts, ideas and reflections to this publication. We acknowledge the support of colleagues at IADT, in the School of Business and Humanities and the National Film School. Finally, we would like to thank our families for their support and patience through each stage of this project.

Acknowledgements

Notes on Contributors

PROF. DESMOND BELL is currently Professor of Film Studies at Queen's University Belfast. Over the last ten years he has written and directed a series of documentary films for television and the cinema, among which his award-winning *Hard Road to Klondike* (1999) and *The Last Storyteller?* (2002) were selected for the Venice Film Festival. His recent documentaries include *Rebel Frontier* (2004) and *Child of the Dead* (2009).

DR PAT BRERETON is currently Associate Dean for Research in the Faculty of Humanities and Social Science at Dublin City University. His books include *Hollywood Utopia: Ecology in contemporary American cinema* (Intellect Books, 2005), *Continuum Guide to Media Education* (Continuum, 2001) and the *Historical Dictionary of Irish Cinema* (Scarecrow Press, 2007) with Roddy Flynn.

ALAN GILSENAN is a film-maker, writer and theatre director. His films include *The Road To God Knows Where* (1988), *Prophet Songs* (1990), *All Souls' Day* (1997), *Zulu 9* (2001), *Paul Durcan: The dark school* (2007), *Maura's Story* (2002), *The Ghost of Roger Casement* (2002), *Timbuktu* (2004), *The Yellow Bittern: The life and times of Liam Clancy* (2009) as well as the documentary series *The Asylum* (2006), *The Hospice* (2007) and *I See A Darkness* (2010). For the theatre, he has directed his own adaptation of John Banville's *The Book of Evidence* at the Kilkenny Festival and the Gate; Tom Murphy's *The Patriot Game*, *On The Outside* and *On The Inside* as well as Tom MacIntyre's *What Happened Bridget Cleary* at the Abbey; Jean Genet's *The Balcony* and Tennessee Williams' *Small Craft Warnings* at the Focus; Samuel Beckett's *Footfalls* at the Gate and the Barbican; and *Knives In Hens* by David Harrower for Landmark Productions.

DR ALAN GROSSMAN is a lecturer in Ethnographic Media Production in the Centre for Transcultural Research and Media Practice, Dublin Institute of Technology. He has published in numerous journals including *Space and Culture* and the *Journal of Ethnic and Migration Studies*, and is co-editor with Áine O'Brien of a book/DVD-ROM publication titled *Projecting Migration: Transcultural Documentary Practice* (Wallflower Press, 2007). His co-directed ethnographic films, *Silent Song* (2000), *Here To Stay* (2006) and *Promise and*

Unrest (2010), have been screened nationally and internationally, and he is currently guest co-editing a forthcoming issue of the *Journal of Media Practice* 9, 2 (2011).

MÁIRE KEARNEY is a producer/director with RTÉ. She started her career with RTÉ's current affairs department in 1992. She subsequently worked for the BBC, TV3 and in the independent sector before returning to RTÉ current affairs in 2004. She won Irish Film & Television Awards (IFTAs) for Best Current Affairs for two of her *Prime Time Investigates* programmes – *Home Truths* in 2005 and *Not Seen, Not Heard* in 2007.

LOUIS LENTIN is executive producer/director with Crescendo Concepts, a leading independent production company, for whom his numerous television documentaries include *Dear Daughter* (1996), *Stolen Lives* (1999), *No More Blooms* (1997), *Ar Dover Féin* (2001); the drama series *Scealta Ó Theach na mBocht* and the food and hospitality series *McKenna's Ireland*. Previously as Head of Drama at RTÉ he produced and directed many notable dramas including Eugene McCabe's *King of the Castle* (1977) and Maeve Binchy's *Deeply Regretted By* (1978), along with the 1916 commemoration series *Insurrection*. His recent documentary *Grandpa Speak to Me in Russian* (2007) has been shown at film festivals worldwide. He is currently working with author Eugene McCabe on a feature film, *Heaven Lies About Us*, based on McCabe's short story of the same title.

RACHEL LYSAGHT is Lead Producer at Underground Films, and a graduate of EAVE and the Samuel Beckett School of Drama, Trinity College Dublin. Her titles include *Identities* (2008), *Joyriders* (2006), *Muide Éire, Jericho* (2009) and *Hum* (2010). Rachel has won many national and international awards – Sapporo International Film Festival, Japan; Festival de Lyon-Villeurbanne, France; Best Documentary Film, Irish Film & Television Awards; Best First Irish Short, Galway Film Fleadh; Gradam Gael Linn, Cork Film Festival. Recently, *Jericho and Hum* was nominated for the Berlin Today Awards, Berlinale 2010. *The Pipe* (2010), which Rachel produced, scooped Best Documentary Film awards at the IFTAs, Galway Film Fleadh and Foyle Film Festival, and an Honourable Mention from the International Documentary Film Festival Amsterdam (IDFA) jury in 2010 and 2011.

RUTH LYSAGHT teaches Media Studies and Irish Cinema at the Université de Bretagne Occidentale, France. She recently completed her PhD (a comparative study of Māori Television and TG4) at the University of Auckland, New Zealand. She has worked in theatre, film and television as writer, script supervisor and researcher, and is currently developing a book about Irish language short films.

DR CAROL MACKEOGH lectures in Media Studies at the Institute of Art, Design and Technology in Dún Laoghaire, Co. Dublin. She is the author of *Participant*

Observation: A team study of young people and television (Dublin: SAI, 2002) and a number of reports/presentations for government agencies on media and young people (Irish Film Classifications Office, Crisis Pregnancy Agency, Internet Advisory Board). Carol worked as a senior researcher with the Centre for Society, Technology & Media at Dublin City University and has also worked in television production as a research/producer with Fastnet Films.

DR CAHAL MCLAUGHLIN is a senior lecturer at the School of Media, Film and Journalism at the University of Ulster. He is a film-maker and writer, director of the *Prisons Memory Archive* and Chair of the Editorial Board of the *Journal of Media Practice*. His most recent publication is *Recording Memories from Political Conflict: A film-maker's journey* (Intellect, 2010).

ALAN MAHER joined the Irish Film Board in 2006. Prior to this, he was Head of Development with Element Pictures. Alan has had particular responsibility for documentaries at the Board and recent films he has exec'd include: *Knuckle* (Sundance Film Festival, 2011); *The Pipe* (Toronto International Film Festival, 2010; Honourable Mention Green Screen IDFA 2010); *His & Hers* (Winner, Best Cinematography World Documentary, Sundance 2010; highest grossing Irish theatrical documentary to date); and *Colony* (Winner IDFA first Appearance Award 2009; Toronto International Film Festival 2009).

JOLENE MAIRS is a PhD student at the Centre for Media Research at the University of Ulster, where she is researching into narrative structure and post-production in the *Prisons Memory Archive* (www.prisonsmemoryarchive.com). Jolene has an MA in Documentary Practice and an MA in Social Work.

DR HARVEY O'BRIEN teaches Film Studies at University College Dublin. He is the author of *The Real Ireland: The evolution of Ireland in documentary film* (Manchester, 2004) and co-editor of *Keeping it Real: Irish film and television* (Wallflower, 2004). He is co-editor of the journal *Film and Film Culture* and the author of numerous articles and book chapters, in addition to having an extensive back catalogue of film and theatre reviews. He is a member of the Board of Directors of the Irish Film Institute and a former Associate Director of the Boston Irish Film Festival.

DR DÍÓG O'CONNELL lectures in film and media at the Institute of Art, Design and Technology in Dún Laoghaire, Co. Dublin. Her book *New Irish Storytellers: Narrative strategies in film* was published by Intellect Press in 2010. She has trained in television production and post-production and has worked in television and film production on a freelance basis. She was a member of the Writers' Team for *Glenroe* (rural-based soap opera) from 1997 to 2001. She has a PhD from Dublin City University in Irish Cinema and has written extensively on this topic.

DR KEVIN RAFTER is a writer and lecturer in politics and media. He is the author of histories of Fine Gael, Sinn Féin and Clann na Poblachta, and is the editor of *Irish Journalism Before Independence: More a disease than a profession* (Manchester University Press, 2011). He spent over a decade working as a political journalist, including with *The Irish Times*, *The Sunday Times*, the *Sunday Tribune* and RTÉ. He now works as a senior lecturer in the School of Communications at Dublin City University.

MARY RAFTERY is an award-winning journalist and television producer. She is the author of *Suffer The Little Children* (1999), director of a number of key documentaries including *States of Fear* (1999) and *Cardinal Secrets* (2002), and co-scripted *No Escape* (2010), a dramatised account based on the Ryan Report commissioned by the Abbey Theatre.

DONALD TAYLOR BLACK is a documentary film-maker and writer. A former Chairman of Documentary, the MEDIA Project for the Creative Documentary, which was based in Copenhagen, he was also a co-founder of the European Documentary Network. He is Head of the Department of Film & Media at the Institute of Art, Design and Technology in Dún Laoghaire, Co. Dublin and Creative Director of the National Film School. His documentaries include *At the Cinema Palace – Liam O'Leary* (1983); *Irish Cinema: Ourselves alone?* (1995); *Hearts and Souls* (1995); *The Joy* (1997); *David Farrell: Elusive moments* (2008).

JULIAN VIGNOLES has worked in RTÉ for over thirty years. He started as a producer in Radio 2, moving to Radio 1 in 1985. He was series producer of *The Pat Kenny Show* and *Liveline* and a three-times Jacob's Award winner for documentary. He moved to RTÉ Television in 1994, producing in Young Peoples' Programmes, before becoming series producer of *Would You Believe*. He moved to Entertainment in 2002 and was deputy head of the department from 2003 to 2009. He is currently Assistant Commissioning Editor, Factual.

KEN WARDROP is a graduate of National Film School, Institute of Art, Design and Technology in Dún Laoghaire, Co. Dublin. During his time at film school, Ken specialised in directing documentary film. His films include the award-winning shorts *Love is Like a Butterfly* (2004), *Useless Dog* (2004) and *The Herd* (2008). His graduation film *Undressing My Mother* (2004) was a multiple award winner. He has co-founded the production company Venom Film with his former classmate Andrew Freedman and is director and editor of *His & Hers* (2010).

PROF. BRIAN WINSTON was the first Lincoln Chair of Communications at the University of Lincoln, United Kingdom. He is the author of a number of books including *Media Technology and Society* (Routledge, 1998), *Lies, Damn Lies and Documentaries* (British Film Institute, 2000), *Messages* (Routledge, 2005). He is the scriptwriter of *A Boatload of Wild Irishmen* (2009) – directed by Mac Dara O Curraidhín – a documentary on Robert Flaherty (TG4/IFB/BAI).

Foreword

This is a remarkable book, a coherent collection of essays and interviews which gives, not a snapshot but a detailed three-dimensional picture of the state of the documentary film in Ireland. It arises from the 2007 documentary conference, organised jointly by the School of Business and Humanities and the National Film School at the Institute of Art, Design and Technology, Dún Laoghaire (IADT), which brought together film-makers, academics (often also film-makers) and funders – a thing seldom done. And this book reflects that comprehensiveness and expands on it. It covers the waterfront – industrial level analysis as well as personal accounts of film-making; the *causes célèbres* and the less contentious output; the impact of technological and social developments. It wears its learning lightly. One might have thought that this combination of approaches was so self-evident for a conference, or a report surveying a national documentary scene, that it would be a commonplace; but it is not. Such a broad range is seldom tackled at the same meeting or between the same covers; and rarely so succinctly and in such a well-focused manner.

Documentary in a Changing State does what it is says on the tin: by examining a communications mode that speaks to the heart of the social agenda, it not only explains Irish documentary but also offers insights into the Irish state as well. Documentary in Ireland has a force which it perhaps lacks in some other societies where authority has learned to cope with its criticisms by, basically, ignoring them. Here is the background to the films that have shaken the country's central institutions. The Irish film-makers have not shirked from investigating history and current problems, the two things that documentary in the realist tradition is paramount at dealing with. They have not sought refuge, as well they might, in dealing only with the soft subjects. This book offers a record of this not inconsiderable achievement and the context in which it happened. It also, therefore, bears witness to the enlightened funding structures that enabled the films to be made (and, of course, to inhibiting factors as well).

Documentarists have a somewhat glib repertoire of justifications for their work which are trotted out in the event that their films cause trouble. This professional litany includes the public's right to know, giving voice to the voiceless, exercising free expression and so on. Often such rhetoric sounds self-serving and patronising because the work is really nothing more than voyeuristic sensationalism. But that is not the case here. From church untouchables to political double standards, Irish documentaries have brought a commendably unflinching gaze to bear. It is, of course, possible to complain that more could and should have been done but, comparatively speaking, what has been made is, in the circumstances, pretty remarkable. The archive of films analysed in *Documentary in a Changing State* represents a glowing testimonial to documentary's essential purpose – to impact on the collective 'mind of a generation', as John Grierson, the Scottish founder of the British documentary film movement, put it some seventy years ago.

Despite the pioneering work of some scholars (who are well represented here), there is still insufficient recognition of the Irish documentary story. That Irish documentaries can now hold their own on the world stage by winning important international prizes is as little generally acknowledged as is their impact on the domestic Irish scene. *Documentary in a Changing State*, building on this earlier work, further corrects that situation. One's only worry is that this ought to be another in an ongoing series of examinations, not an epitaph for a somewhat golden age.

Prof. Brian Winston

Introduction
Documentary in a
changing state

CAROL MACKEOGH AND DÍÓG O'CONNELL

The Role of Documentary in the Public Sphere

Fifty years ago, when Radio Telefís Éireann (RTÉ) first came on air, the media was seen as the handmaiden of the state. Censorship was considered a proper and positive aspect of good governance and, through the close relationship with the state, the media was by and large compliant and obedient.[1] The media's role was to support the state, the church and big business; to maintain the status quo. It was certainly not to investigate, challenge or criticise. There was a deep suspicion and distrust of investigative documentaries. When 7 Days (1966–76), one of the first major current affairs productions on RTÉ, broadcast a programme exploring the practice of money lending in 1969, it became a national scandal. Following debate in the Dáil, a tribunal of inquiry was established to investigate, not money lending, but the way the documentary was made, particularly the use of hidden cameras and microphones.[2]

Now, in a more stable democracy, the balance has shifted and the media play a key role as the watchdog of society.[3] We have become accustomed to a wide variety of methods being used to investigate illegal and immoral activities. As a media-literate society we are used to ministers, church leaders and corporate bosses being interviewed rigorously. Most important of all, such is the impact of media messages such as television documentaries that they can often compel powerful institutions to make public apologies and to change their policies and practices. In 2005, after a Prime Time investigation into the care of the elderly in nursing homes, the then taoiseach Bertie Ahern was forced to announce that legislation was being prepared to establish a Health Information Quality Authority and a Social Services Inspectorate. Again, the taoiseach acknowledged the role of the media when he credited an earlier production, the documentary Dear Daughter (1996), with obliging the government to respond to abuses of power in religious and state-run educational institutions.[4]

In both these instances, the state was compelled to respond to accusations of malpractice arising from investigative television programmes. In the 1990s,

1

it was a television documentary that led to the establishment of the Beef Tribunal and a state investigation as to how the barons of corporate Ireland operated.[5] However, it is the shift in balance of power between the Catholic Church and the media which has been the most dramatic.[6] Of all the institutional powers in Ireland, the church had managed to stay out of the media spotlight. However, a number of path-breaking television documentaries which revealed systemic failures in protecting children from abusive members of the clergy meant that the church also had to be accountable to the people of Ireland via the media.

Habermas has pointed to the key role of the media in the development of a public space, independent of church and state, where citizens can voice opinions and debate issues of general interest. Tracing this media intervention back to eighteenth-century coffee houses, he writes about this space as '. . . a realm in our social life in which something approaching public opinion can be formed'.[7] While he has questioned the wider media landscape that has evolved since those early days, and strongly critiqued the impact of commodification, there is evidence that some of the media can still play a crucial role in the development of a mature and critically informed public sphere. In this book we look, in particular, to the documentaries (both stand-alone and forming part of current affairs coverage) that contributed to a questioning of a range of cultural, economic and political structures. Rather than remain in the midst of a romantic Ireland, where injustice was perpetrated by aberrant individuals – the 'bad apples' in the barrel – these documentaries began to question the very structures of society.

There was a sustained passage of time, at the end of the last millennium, when many 'bad apples' fell off Irish institutional trees. Our trust in the judicial system and the role of the Gardaí as the upholders of justice was undermined by scandals such as the 'Kerry Babies' and McBrearty cases, while a series of malpractices, such as the 'Hep C' and Neary cases, dented the confidence of the public in the medical profession.[8] Politics has also been undermined. We discovered that politicians are adept at double standards in relation to their private lives and, as the recent findings from the Moriarty Tribunal into payments to politicians has shown, many have engaged in corruption and developed cosy, mutually rewarding relations with big business.[9]

Finally, even before the revelations of child sexual abuse, the Catholic Church had come in for scrutiny, first through uncovering that Bishop Éamon Casey and Fr Michael Cleary were not only having sex outside marriage, significant in the context of vows of celibacy, but had fathered children, stories that were broken publicly in the early 1990s. Far more seriously, we learned from the Ryan and Murphy reports of the horrendous regimes of rape, torture, and mental and physical abuse that operated in industrial and reformatory schools.

It must be remembered, then, that the television documentaries that began to emerge during the 1990s were part of a new culture and civil society. There was more questioning, more doubt, and increasingly less confidence in institutions and authority figures. Other key elements in this coming of age of Ireland include the fusion of the traditional and local with a more global and cosmopolitan culture. Peace in Northern Ireland loosened entrenched positions and allowed for debate that was no longer dominated by nationalist issues and, as discussed further below, allowed for the removal of a draconian censorship that had curtailed the media.

Another factor was the diminishing inequality between men and women, represented by the election of two female presidents, Mary Robinson (1990) and Mary McAleese (1997), both of whom cut across formal, official protocols and spoke with a new sincerity and integrity. Our membership of the European Union played a crucial role in the processes of modernisation at economic, social and political levels,[10] but perhaps most noticeably through high-profile legal cases heard in the European Court of Human Rights.[11] Finally, economic policies that invested heavily in education created a work force that saw Ireland 'leap-frog' industrialisation and move from a predominantly agricultural base to an information society.[12] The rapid economic growth that took place from the mid-1990s enabled increased travel, exposure to cultures abroad and, particularly through the internet, access to new knowledge and ideas which, along with increased immigration, contributed to a growing sense of multi-culturalism.

The media played an important role in furthering these processes of change by focusing public attention on key issues and legitimising modernisation. Unlike fictional accounts, current affairs is governed by legislation; it is seen to speak the 'truth' and, unlike other media, television impacts on a wide public. Of course, as Harvey O'Brien notes in his book *The Real Ireland: The Evolution of Ireland in Documentary Film*, this exercise of investigative documentary is a fairly recent practice, and not all of those documentaries that prised open Irish society were made by Irish media.[13] But the reasons for this late flowering, which are manifold, is a recurring theme in this book as our writers reflect on their role in the story of Irish documentary. Our contributors are not representative of all documentary makers and commentators in their field, but are some of the key voices that have questioned Irish society, Irish broadcasting structures and the characteristics of the documentary form. The remainder of this Introduction maps out the frameworks in which they have operated – the historical background and evolving broadcast landscape, and the changing nature of documentary formats and audience expectations – followed by a brief overview of the sections and chapters in the book.

Documentary on Irish Television: historical perspective

From the setting up of RTÉ television in 1961 – one of the off-shoots of the modernisation project undertaken by Seán Lemass and T.K. Whitaker – to the 1980s when RTÉ underwent radical reform at institutional level, Ireland's transformation has been well reflected by Irish television, though not always within the current affairs format.[14] In the 1970s particularly, as the forces for change met with traditional values, it was television drama and sometimes light entertainment (*The Late Late Show*) that played the main role in charting the tensions in Irish society.[15] Through drama, issues were exposed that could not be addressed directly in factual programming. *The Late Late Show* often brought opposing forces together or interviewed controversial figures, and would generate debate beyond the programme itself. Tracking developments in documentary up until the 1980s, Harvey O'Brien concludes that 'Irish documentaries remained unable to examine, explore or otherwise envision the present in the kinds of terms which observational documentaries had done and were doing in the United States and elsewhere'.[16]

Some notable exceptions however did tackle issues such as abuse in Irish society, even though these revelations did not always capture the popular imagination at the time. In 1981 Cathal Black produced the drama documentary *Our Boys* exploring physical abuse in a Christian Brothers-run institution. It was banned at the time by RTÉ and not screened in Ireland until 1991. *A Week in the Life of Martin Cluxton* (1971), a drama documentary in the style of Ken Loach's *Cathy Come Home* (1966), told the story of a juvenile released from a borstal after a two-year sentence for a minor misdemeanour. This film acts as an inquiry into who is responsible for the welfare of young people who are drifting towards the edge. It is a critically reflective documentary which, ultimately, lays the blame at the state's door.[17]

While there were pockets of more radical voices, RTÉ as an institution of the state endorsed censorship, secrecy and curbing freedom of speech. Irish documentary was underdeveloped because of lack of funds and poor equipment but primarily because of a 'pervasive insular conservatism' which dominated early productions.[18] RTÉ was also legally bound by Section 31 of the Broadcasting Act (1960), a legislative form of censorship that prevented broadcast media interviewing members of various organisations, Sinn Féin, the IRA and so forth, but which resulted in the silencing of oppositional voices in areas beyond those of national security. For a journalist and documentary maker attempting to cover the Troubles in Northern Ireland over a thirty-year period, this piece of legislation ensured that it was very difficult to get to the heart of a story.[19] At the same time, the institutional approach in RTÉ went further, employing self-censorship and/or actively discouraging these stories being told. The legacy is an enormous black hole in the archives. With the exception of a reportage approach, through the formats of news and current affairs, the story of the Troubles goes untold outside of foreign productions. This had a knock-on effect – how could documentary makers begin to tackle other issues – social, economic or cultural – when they were hindered in representing unfolding political events in their own country? It is no wonder that Irish documentary has an impoverished history compared to the challenging stories that its diaspora tackled.[20] It could be added that, along with a poor legacy of documenting our own history and current affairs, it was an even rarer occurrence to document social or political events in other countries from an Irish perspective. One documentary strand does stand out – *Radharc* (established in 1961) managed to voice a radical view 'under the radar' of the state and the church hierarchy probably because it was produced by Catholic priests. It critiqued injustice not just in Irish society but also in other countries. More recently, Irish documentary makers have begun to travel abroad and none perhaps more dramatically than the crew that witnessed and reported on the coup in Venezuela in *Chávez: The Revolution Will Not Be Broadcast*.[21]

While the legal and political constraints persisted, the 1980s was a key decade for Irish television particularly in relation to the development of private sector broadcasting. The world of broadcasting at EU level was undergoing radical changes as a result of developments in technology (such as satellite, VCR, the move away from film stock) and the increasing pressure to deregulate the market. While the legislation to facilitate this in Ireland was not passed until the 1988 and 1990 Broadcasting Acts, the internal reorganisation of RTÉ and the broadcasting landscape was already under way. It could be argued that the most significant event for the changing face of documentary production in Ireland can be traced back to 1985 and the publication of a consultants' report by Stokes Kennedy Crowley (SKC). This report recommended, among other things, greater activity in co-productions and international sales and, most significantly, that RTÉ would be obliged to commission and broadcast a quota of programming material from outside the institution.[22] Providing the economic infrastructure for a broader range of programme making activity, this development gave birth to the independent sector and sowed the seeds for the emergence of the Independent Production Unit (IPU) within RTÉ. Initially, many of those who provided programme material from the newly developed independent sector were producers and directors who took the opportunity offered by redundancy from RTÉ to set up their own production companies. Mike Murphy, Larry Masterson, John McColgan and Gerry Gregg among others would form the backbone of the early independent sector. Gradually, producers and directors would emerge who did not cut their teeth in RTÉ and, as Mary Raftery notes in Section IV of this book, this process was key to transforming the cultural face of Irish documentary.

At a national level, the 1988 and 1990 Broadcasting Acts set about dismantling RTÉ's dominance of the market and reducing its public service remit. For the first time RTÉ would have direct competition from within the national territory as well as having to commission from the independent sector.[23] Farrel Corcoran argues that some of the most profound changes in broadcasting in Ireland took place in the 1990s.[24] In relation to television, these changes included the 'establishment of the Irish-language television channel Teilifís na Gaeilge in 1996 (now TG4), the arrival of the Canadian-based multinational television company CanWest in Ireland as a major force in the launch of TV3 in 1998 (to be followed by Granada as co-owner), and the development of a national strategy for digital television'.[25]

Following the Broadcasting Act of 2009, the title of Authority, and the regulatory power that went with the title, passed from RTÉ to the Broadcasting Authority of Ireland (BAI). This new body replaced the Broadcasting Commission of Ireland (BCI) which had broadened its function to include funding opportunities for documentary makers, as well as fiction film, animation and other programme formats. These funding opportunities for documentaries in the independent and community television sector now provide a support outlet for sole documentary producers beyond those offered by RTÉ. A very significant political decision was the re-activation of Bord Scannán na hÉireann (Irish Film Board) in 1993. While the emphasis is on the support for fiction feature film-making, the Board also supports independent documentary making and, in association with the Arts Council, placed a specific emphasis on documenting the arts. Against this background is the European Union's MEDIA programmes and the 'Television without Frontiers' strategy, that provide a range of supports for the audio-visual industry – training, production, distribution and exhibition. The major shifts for the documentary maker over the past thirty years have, then, been in the areas of production finance and exhibition.

So while there can be a tendency to look back to a 'golden age' of public service broadcasting before market liberalisation, there are now, arguably, more opportunities for funding documentary making principally through the growth of the independent sector. However, documentaries, like all other areas of broadcasting, are being forced to manage within much tighter budgets, allowing less time and resources to complete a project. This has been ushered in as a result of technological changes and market liberalisation since the 1980s. The new platforms emerging in the form of digital and internet technology are offering alternatives to the mainstream, particularly evident in the changes in education and training for media.

In the social and political turmoil of the past thirty years, Irish documentary makers have not remained silent but have exploited many of the opportunities in a global market to get their stories produced. Of all audio-visual formats, it could be argued that the documentary form has kept pace with changes in technology and infrastructure which are reflected not so much in the way the stories are told, but how they are exhibited and disbursed to more fragmented and diverse audiences.

Documentary Formats and Audience Expectations

This book is, in part, a celebration of the media – and documentary media in particular – as a force that has, if only recently, helped Irish society change its ideas and own up to its past. But it is also about putting the media in perspective. Inasmuch as we have begun to question other institutions, so too we need to question the role of the media. Do they have the power to decide on the issues that need addressing, to set the agenda for public debate? Or do they, as they themselves might claim, merely reflect the issues that emerge within society? And, in either case – whether they lead or follow – how ought the media reflect on that role and tackle questions of objectivity and bias?

While we might often hear about the power of the media and their impact *on* society, there is ample evidence that they can only succeed in setting the agenda because they tune into the ongoing issues and concerns of their audiences – those that arise *from* society. They may play a role in planting the seeds of those issues, but unless people are ready for new ideas, unless they are able to reflect on, talk about and conceptualise current problems, the messages of the media will fall on deaf ears. The church scandals are a case in point. There were, as mentioned above, earlier reports and documentaries that revealed institutional abuse, but they were not received with the same mass response that *Dear Daughter* (1996) and *States of Fear* (1999) provoked. It was only later that the time was right for these documentaries. Up until then, people did not have the language to comprehend or respond to the issues and the scale of the problem. Neither did many programme controllers have the courage to back the documentary makers and take on the Catholic Church. Like many others, they showed deference to the church and conceptualised clerical child sexual abuse as isolated cases or part of the 'bad apple' syndrome. A more recent case in point is the current affairs programmes and documentaries that warned of the demise of the Celtic Tiger. Caught in a frenzy of consumer spending, many of us were unable or unwilling to listen to those that forecast economic doom. Rather than the media simply setting the agenda for public debate, the process is a more flexible and dynamic one as the media must link in with the *zeitgeist* in which they operate.

If our documentary makers are tuning into anxieties and problems that emerge in society, are they then simply the conduits that reveal what those issues are? Are they simply neutral 'windows' on to the world? Most commentators on documentary point to the genre's special connection to 'reality' or 'actuality' and the audience expectation that documentaries are based on facts.[26] However, those writers also point out that all media communicate by way of representation which, of its nature, entails processes of selection and construction that tend to undermine any notion of 'truth'. Events and issues have to be encoded into words and images that will translate meaningfully for an audience. As with all forms of representation, documentary must use accepted codes and conventions to create that sense of 'reality' or 'actuality' – codes and conventions which feed into audiences' expectations. But while documentary is expected to be based in fact or actuality, it differs from current affairs in that it is given more licence to place those facts into narratives.[27] Documentary has been defined as 'the creative treatment of actuality' and the definition of what counts as 'creativity' has been a key ethical issue in the field.[28] While journalists may be advised to seek out content that could be considered factual and to separate this from opinion or belief, it is not so easy to define a similar ethic in documentary. If, as the key theorists have pointed out, documentaries are, of their nature, constructions that entail imaginative elements, it may be preferable that this is spelled out rather than hidden behind veneers of objectivity.[29]

Brian Winston, who contributes the foreword to this book, has argued that the 'creative' aspect of documentary has become tied up in regulations as the genre has become confused with factual programming.[30] In some cases the 'creativity' has been mistaken for 'fakery', in, for example, the use of reconstructions – as if live action footage was in some way less mediated. This has been at the expense of focusing on what perhaps should be the key ethical concern for documentary makers – their relationship with those that they are documenting. If this was the case, then the integrity of documentaries would depend more on the careful consideration of issues around informed consent and participation. This topic comes alive in many of the chapters in this book – particularly in Alan Gilsenan's contribution – as the documentary makers chart their relationships in the field and the dilemmas they faced in balancing the human cost of documentary making with the demands for new and innovative ways to tell stories.

Documentary in a Changing State sets out, then, to look at the changing state of documentary as a form of communication. In some ways it too has lost some of its authority and credibility. Fifty years ago, documentaries were predominantly what Nichols called 'expository'.[31] As envisaged by Grierson – who is credited with coining the term – they were intended to be educative and didactic; a lynchpin in the development of an informed public, capable of living in democratic systems.[32] Expository documentaries had very clear messages to impart, initially from one point of view only, and delivered by voice-over, usually an authoritative, upper-class, male voice. It was as if God was using the airwaves to speak to his people. These conventions may have persuaded the audience that they were listening to the truth, viewing actuality.

Now, if we heard the heavy pronouncements of those early documentary voice-overs, we might think that it was a joke, a *Monty Python* take-off of 'a very important message'. The rhetoric has changed and, there too, our levels of credibility have shifted. Now we expect testimony from witnesses and first-hand accounts from authentic participants – conventions more in keeping with the era of reality television. But again, reality television did not appear out of nowhere. Inasmuch as it may be claiming to reflect 'actual' lives, it also feeds into the expectations that audiences bring to bear – new sets of codes and conventions that are designed to address a society that has precisely lost faith in the ability of any institution to speak the truth.

Critical Reflections on Documentary

This collection of essays brings together a range of participants in Irish documentary film-making who have reflected personally on their role and experiences in the field. The writing styles and approaches are eclectic – reflecting the varied backgrounds of the contributors as documentary makers who are also academics, educationalists, policy makers, and journalists. The book is divided into four sections to reflect the varied backgrounds of the contributors but there is a common theme of exploring documentary practice from the insider perspective.

The *academe* has had a growing preoccupation with bringing theory and practice closer together across many disciplines in the past decade. No longer are the voices of media theorists seen as credible if they are wholly removed from practitioners and their performance. At the same time, the student of production techniques is often informed by a variety of theoretical approaches designed to encourage critical engagement and reflection with their own practice. This book is designed to explore the ongoing discourse and relationship between theory and practice.

Section I of the book contains contributions from documentary makers who are also working as academics and have reflected on and questioned documentary form. Harvey O'Brien, leading academic expert on Irish documentary, sets the tone for critical interrogation in his introductory piece to this section. Setting the bar high for the potential of the documentary to interrogate and intervene in a changing society, he suggests that, taken as a whole, the practice in Ireland hasn't gone far enough, while acknowledging some notable contributors to the field, many of whom write essays for this volume. Alan Grossman engages with the debates around ethnographic and socially engaged documentary and, through an examination of his own approach, reflects on the varied ways of categorising and engaging with diversity. He poses the question as to whether documentary can 'prise open a critical and reflective space', which might contribute to a 'living archive' of the migration experience in its multiplicity of constructions. Similarly exploring new experiences, Cahal McLaughlin and Jolene Mairs address collaborative film-making and the use of archives, recording and memory production in post-conflict Ireland. These writers recount a specific approach to reflective practice which seeks to accommodate a diversity of experience, previously seen in terms of opposition across a political divide. Through their project they uncover many points of commonality. Concluding this section, Desmond Bell teases out the relationship of history to documentary film in a new and original way. In exploring how to achieve dramatic reconstruction of the past for film, Bell discusses archival film, the voice-over and reconstructed sequences and reveals the thinking behind key decisions that were taken in the production context of some of his own specific works.

Section II contains reflective personal accounts by dedicated practitioners who have been addressing key social issues. Alan Gilsenan, Louis Lentin, Julian Vignoles and Máire Kearney discuss how their own documentary programmes and films impacted dramatically on Irish society in the past twenty years. Alan Gilsenan examines the ethical dilemmas that the documentary maker must face and, through his own experience, explores the contradictions in the official approach to the process and the personal responsibility that emerges in real situations. Louis Lentin's *Dear Daughter* (1996) lifted the lid of secrecy on institutional abuse and allowed for the flood gates to open to personal stories of lost childhood and emotional, psychological and physical abuse at the hands of the religious orders. His essay details the production context and constraints in getting those stories told. It vividly chronicles the various obstacles that must be overcome by a documentary maker struggling for time, space, resources and supports for stories that need to be told. Similarly, Máire Kearney's case study approach discusses the production methods involved in breaking taboos, exposing double standards and getting behind the scenes of institutions of care in contemporary Ireland. As a series producer, Julian Vignoles reflects on the working environment of the documentary maker who seeks to tell stories about modern, contemporary Ireland, sometimes within conservative and conventional formats but also within practical constraints of time and budget. He shows how those formats can be renegotiated in order to push the boundaries of representation. Together, these essays offer unique insights into the workings of documentary film-making whether it is on the periphery of independent production or centrally institutionalised within a public service operation.

A number of different perspectives on aspects of policy and development are explored in Section III. It provides a historical overview of the key changes in documentary production during the past twenty years, resulting from structural changes in the broadcast landscape. Donald Taylor Black explores the path of the independent producer and director and the tensions between the commissioners and the documentary maker working through what is, often, a site of conflicting opinion and practice. Through an empirical study of the relationship between the IPU in RTÉ and the independent sector, Kevin Rafter explores how definitions of documentary often change and evolve within a political and economic context rather than according to the narrative and aesthetic norms of the format itself. Using statistical data, Rafter gives an overview of the field from the rationale of the policy maker. Rachel and Ruth Lysaght celebrate the achievement of documentary within TG4, a branch of public service broadcasting operating outside the dominant paradigm. Rather than this being a disadvantage, they explore how it has distinguished this service, particularly through the production supports it offers for documentary form, and how it has linked to other cultures through its peripheral status. Looking to the future, and the landscape of education, training and practice that is unfolding for the next generation of documentary makers, Pat Brereton details new platforms and outlines the potential for achieving alternative spaces for exhibition and audience links, mainly through new technologies.

The concluding section of the book presents three interviews conducted with documentary maker Ken Wardrop (*His & Hers*, 2010), journalist Mary Raftery (*States of Fear*, 1999) and policy maker and production executive Alan Maher (Irish Film Board/Bord Scannán na hÉireann). These interviews round off the approach, adopted from the outset, of exploring the three areas of theory, practice and policy that have informed documentary making in Ireland in recent times.

This book is designed to ensure a wide-ranging discussion among academics, practitioners and policy makers, and to produce a resource for undergraduate and postgraduate students in the field of media and film studies. It is also designed to inform a general audience interested in the role documentary has made in tracking and facilitating a changing Irish society – politically, socially and culturally – since the 1990s. The art form of documentary acts as a prism through which these key moments in recent Irish history are negotiated and revealed so that shedding light on this process can inform our understanding of the nature of these changes.

previous experience with the media and very comfortably guided us around his boxing club, keen to show how he had re-built the club over many years. This sense of co-ownership of re-telling the participants' stories as they wanted to tell them was a vital component of our collaborative approach. While this approach allows for transparency of the film-making process between film-makers and participants, it also provides an opportunity for compromise when contrasting agendas between the different producers arise.

Representation

The collaboration with WAVE provoked several discussions about our different –sometimes overlapping, sometimes contrasting – agendas. After the first public screening, WAVE asked for a photograph to be placed at the beginning of each story of the person who had died along with a text-box giving their name, date of death and the organisation responsible for the death. Working with the material that we had been given by the participants, there was an inevitable unevenness to their information. For example, not all had mentioned the organisation responsible for the death. WAVE operates in a political terrain where some victims' and survivors' groups, as well as political parties, contest the category of 'victim', describing some as 'innocent' and some, such as ex-prisoners, as 'perpetrators'. Not surprisingly, many victims' and survivors' groups are geographically based and, given the persistent segregation of communities despite the peace process, few are able to represent outside of their immediate political or spatial communities. WAVE is the largest such representative group and has five centres across Northern Ireland. They are scrupulous about their openness to all who have suffered. This inclusiveness is a condition of being seen to be impartial and balanced.

As film-makers, we were interested in the idea of approaching the theme of loss by using the present to look at the past. Memory, while looking back, is a phenomenon of the present and conditioned by these circumstances. People remember differently, not only over time, but also depending on the psychic and physical spaces that are inhabited. We were interested in how and what people remembered. We were also interested in transcending differences of affiliation, whether political, social or religious. We wished to ask audiences to privilege the human story over the political context, to suspend judgement on who was responsible until empathy had been considered for the person surviving. Part of our reasoning was that the requirement to understand the 'other' is a crucial aspect of the peace process. We hoped audiences would first listen to the story of loss and survival and later connect or challenge this experience with their subject positions of being nationalist or unionist or any other position. The information that the six participants came from 'both' communities was required by WAVE to be signalled up front and this was not clearly evident on first viewing. A compromise was reached when we agreed to use the photographs, but asked the participants to say in their own words who they felt was responsible for the deaths of their loved ones. While this may work against our own desire to move beyond labels, the work that WAVE is doing, in a public arena of contestation and political conflict, requires our appreciation.

Exhibition

Since completing production of *Unheard Voices* in March 2009, we have to date held five public screenings of the film in various locations around Northern Ireland. Prior to the public screenings we held a private screening for the participants and family and friends only. This allowed them to see the film collectively as a group for the first time and provided them with an additional opportunity to have their film removed from the final edit or to have any alterations made to their film. The participants saw how their stories were positioned within the overall structure of the film and the film-makers were able to explain in detail our methodology, including the post-production of the material. There was a general sense of satisfaction with the result and the discussion led to plans for distribution of the work.

At the public screenings the film-makers and participants offered a panel discussion with the audience afterwards. Mike Nesbitt, one of the four victims commissioners appointed by the first and deputy first minister, chaired the proceedings. Beginning with a question from a DUP elected representative about forgiveness, the panel took it in turns to discuss the issues that the film raised. There was little said about the process of the film-making, which could be read as a positive sign that the participants had used the film and its production process to develop their ideas and feelings about their loss. One comment from Pat McCauley seemed to validate our methodology: 'A few weeks ago, I would not have anticipated that they [the participants] would be sitting up here articulating their feelings so clearly. Making this film has added immensely to their confidence.' This was confirmed at a final, closed residential event following the public screening, where several participants echoed Pat's views. Sandra stated that she felt 'complete and utter shock at being able to do it. I couldn't believe I had done it. Even to speak in public was some achievement.'

Conclusion

We set out to create a framework in which a small group of victims and survivors of the Troubles had the opportunity to tell their stories in a process that provided safety and support; where they remained authors of their own stories; where public acknowledgement of their trauma would be offered; and where the issues raised could be discussed more widely.

The film addresses issues that the victims and survivors struggle with on a daily basis: traumatic bereavement, loss, and lack of closure and justice. The participants' responses suggest that the recording methodologies adopted in the creation of *Unheard Voices* were positive. There is some evidence in their responses that the process of creating an audio-visual recording was difficult, but beneficial. Lorna described having 'a feeling of achievement' at having completed her film. Mark stated how he found it very encouraging to 'witness the growth within individuals' as they went through the process of telling their story. Paul also described 'a sense of achievement that we all took part in it and getting a platform to share what happened to me'.

However, we must remain cautious about the potential of the above process to be extended unchanged. In a society where division is still embedded in the fabric of the geographical, educational and political landscape, where political violence persists, either at the level of the street or in paramilitary attacks, recalling and recounting our memories of trauma may not always receive the welcome that *Unheard Voices* has so far received. Where one person's 'victim' may be another's 'perpetrator', where a hierarchy of victims is being sought in the legislation (albeit unlikely to receive the necessary cross-party support), where attempts at alleviation of pain run up against the risk of re-stimulation of pain, then each political and psychic circumstance of community, group and individual will need to be addressed in future filmmaking of this genre. We hope that we have at least laid down some guidelines that might be useful to others who plan to develop such work.

Documentary Film
and History

DESMOND BELL

Introduction

Documentary films dealing with historical subjects are increasingly popular
with audiences. They have of course always been a stable of public service
broadcasting. Now within the proliferating world of cable and satellite television we have specialist channels exclusively concerned with history
programming such as the History Channel and a number of others, for
example Discovery and National Geographic, with a substantial percentage of
such programming. How do documentary film-makers picture the past and
in what ways does their approach differ from the orthodox writing of history?[1]
Is the documentary a populist form which necessarily involves the 'dumbing
down' of academic history? On the other hand, can the inclusion of historical
documentary material within the television schedule extend access to historical understanding to a broader range of people than the specialist texts of
academic written history?

In this paper I draw upon my own work as a documentary film-maker
concerned with historical issues to explore some of the ways film- and
programme-makers have dealt with problems of historical representation and
narrative.

The Historian's Scepticism towards Film

From the outset let us admit that historians have a deep suspicion towards the
notion that film-making might represent a methodologically valid way to 'do'
history. And yet, historians and documentarists by and large share a commitment to an ethic of public communication with its attendant notion of truth
and impartiality. However, historians remain suspicious of the epistemolog-
ical status and cultural role of documentary film. Many have concerns about
the evidential status of the forms of personal testimony and narrative revelation that documentary films often rely upon. Many are uncomfortable with
the notion of memory as a constitutive concept within historiography and
have remained aloof from the sustained debate about 'popular memory' that
has taken place within critical studies.[2] And this is so despite the development

of oral history approaches within their discipline and the increasing use of visual sources and media contents as historical data. Historians have, however, been slow to engage in the corresponding critical debate around the mediated and contingent nature of collective memory and photographic record.

The scepticism of historians towards film has not of course inhibited historians from offering their services as historical consultants to programme-makers tackling historical subjects. Within the BBC model of the historical documentary the historian-as-consultant functions as a source of 'quality control'. They are brought on board to oversee and underwrite the authenticity of programme content in accordance with the existing state of historical knowledge. Within this Reithian-inspired model historians don't need to know much – or indeed anything – about the programme production process or about the formal features of film.[3] They are hired to vouch for the historical credentials of the piece.

From this perspective the historical documentary can look like an applied and, let's face it, 'second rate' form of doing history. Dependent for its factual accuracy on the mother discipline, the historical documentary film is viewed as an act of communication of previously accredited historical knowledge relayed through a mass medium.

The historians who actually appear in front of camera in historical documentaries have largely approached the challenge of televising history from a pedagogic standpoint, often operating with a model of broadcast documentary as a form of illustrated lecture. The historian/presenter marshals their arguments before the camera and illuminates these employing the visual resources that lens-based media can make available – live-action cinematography revisiting historical sites, dramatic reconstructions of events, expert testimony, use of picture archive, etc. The great masters of this genre were of course A.J.P. Taylor and Kenneth Clarke, who in a simpler television age produced spellbinding performances to camera with relatively few cinematic resources at their disposal.

But the model has tenacity within television. Today Simon Schama has assumed the mantle of the 'history man'. Besides writing the scripts of the series he has been involved with,[4] Schama has also had a significant input into other aspects of some of these productions, including the choice of locations and elements of visualisation strategy. Unlike Taylor and Clarke, Schama in his films has to deal with the indignity of large sections of dramatic reconstruction where out-of-work actors and hapless extras are directed to show us how things looked, felt and indeed *were* in 'olden times'.

Documentarists remain divided about the validity of re-enactment within factual film-making. The problem is that documentary film in its contract with its audience vouches to represent *the* world and not just a fictional construction of *a* world given flesh in the diegesis and design of a film. Yet, no matter how thorough our historical research, in the absence of recorded testimony and preserved image we can only represent the distant past (or indeed any historical period prior to the late nineteenth-century) by making a series of assumptions about this via a filmic diegesis.

Indeed in picturing the past, directors settle for a form of coherent verisimilitude that has little to do with the observational practices of documentary film-making and everything to do with the realist codes of the nineteenth-century novel and the twentieth-century ones of the costume drama. Interestingly, Schama has said that he saw his writing task on the series he has worked on as akin to providing a screenplay. I'll call this approach, found in many historical documentaries, 'unreconstructed reconstruction'. The introduction of 'well-dressed' fictive elements into a documentary film can be a destabilising one. The desire to achieve the 'look' of the past and to hypothesise how people looked, dressed, talked and behaved peddles the illusion that we as audience can directly access the past through the photographic power of the filmic medium. It offers us the illusion that the screen can be an unmediated window on the past showing us 'how it really was'.

Re-enacting History

However, there *are* other ways to do dramatic filmic reconstruction of the past. My first film, *We'll Fight and No Surrender: Ulster Loyalism and the Protestant Sense of History* (1989), and two later ones, *Redeeming History* (1990) and *Out of Loyal Ulster* (1993), sought to engage with popular senses of history in Ireland and their role in the construction of collective identity. This perspective quickly took the film-maker beyond the illustrated lecture model and beyond the faux naturalism of costume drama.

We'll Fight, for example, involves a 'reconstruction' of the iconic moment in loyalist history when the fabled twelve Apprentice Boys of Derry rushed forward to slam the gates of the city in the face of the advancing Jacobite army in December 1688, thereby committing the beleaguered Protestants of Ulster to the Williamite cause.

We 'monkeyed around' with the 'parts'. During the shoot a number of unemployed Catholic young men habitually hung around the walls 'killing time'. We asked them to 'perform' the shutting of the gates event by closing a modern security gate erected by the British Army within the original Magazine Gate of the city and used to control vehicular access to the commercial centre of Derry. This 'live action' material was then intercut with footage shot at a later date of loyalist bands parading at a 'Relief of Derry' commemorative parade. We see the bandsmen advancing in full regalia towards New Gate which leads into the historic centre of the city. In our cut the loyalists 'play the part' of the besieging Jacobite forces while the Apprentice Boys are played by the nationalist youth in a playful reversal of traditional roles.

Fig. 6 Loyalist Band: *We'll Fight and No Surrender*

I guess we were seeking to make past and present collide – not, I might add, in the reassuring formula of Irish revisionist historiography where the professional historian exposes the mythic status and folly of popular and ideologically charged versions of history, loyalist or republican.

In *Redeeming History*, commissioned by Channel 4 Television, we invited a group of Protestant sixth-form pupils from a school in Derry to explore aspects of a radical Protestant tradition. The film explores the period of the Volunteer movement, in particular the political career of one of its leaders, the enigmatic earl bishop of Derry, Frederick Augustus Hervey. As the young people got further into the story of what we can call – for want of a better term – Protestant nationalism, they discovered the difficulties the Volunteers had in accommodating the democratic requirement of Catholic Emancipation within their demands for political autonomy for the Irish parliament. As the project developed, significant differences of opinion appeared within the group of young people. These appeared to relate to contemporary political anxieties and division within the Protestant community. In a key sequence in the film we explored Hervey's failed attempt to convince his fellow Volunteers at the national convention of the movement in Dublin to support the extension of the franchise to their Catholic fellow-nationals.[5]

Radically different filmic elements are brought together to narrate this key episode in Irish history: contemporary footage of a St Patrick's Day parade in Dublin attended by the young Protestants; heated discussions among the pupils on the question of political identity and contemporary republican terrorism. Hervey's impassioned speech to the convention is delivered by actor Stan

Townsend. This performance is intercut with contemporary footage of members of the loyalist Apprentice Boys of Derry burning an effigy of the iconic traitor to the loyalist cause, Robert Lundy, as they do annually every December. Through montage, past and present, fact and myth, ethnographic report and filmic enactment are brought into an expressive alignment. History is grasped as a process of troubling investigation that can lead to communal self-questioning. Our engagement with the past reveals the anxieties and interests of the present.

Historian Robert Rosenstone argues that the experimental history film is a distinctive way of doing history.

> Rather than opening a window directly onto the past [it] opens a window onto a different way of *thinking* about the past. The aim is not to tell everything, but to point to past events, or to converse about history, or to show why history should be meaningful to people in the present.[6]

To 'converse about history' . . . 'to make it meaningful' . . . could these not be common aims for the historian and the film-maker?

Oral history and Visual Record in the Documentary

Documentary film with its power to provide personal witness and to explore memory through our visual archives has contributed to re-establishing the new centrality of the oral and the visual as sources for 'doing history' and perhaps this will be its abiding contribution to the sort of 'postmodern historiography' envisaged by Rosenstone.

In my film *The Last Storyteller? / An Scéalaí Deireanach?* I explored the role of oral record and visual archive in exploring folk memory. This film, made in both English and Irish, follows the life of folklore collector Seán Ó hEochaidh (who died in 1992) and deals with the eclipse of traditional storytelling within Gaelic culture in the twentieth century. However, it also muses on how filmic language – including the evocative power of moving-image archive – might provide a new resource for the re-telling of folk tales and for the exploration of myth as communal narrative. The film retells a number of the classic folk tales Seán collected in Donegal from the 1930s. Fictive elements – footage from Brian Desmond Hurst's 1935 version of *Riders to the Sea* are combined with documentary footage of a 1940s Irish market town and with contemporary live action cinematography to retell a traditional story – *The Cobbler and his Wife*. We explore Donegal folk ways and interrogate myth.

One area where the conversation between historians and film-makers might usefully begin is around the use and interpretation of the archival image. These images, both still and moving, serve as both testimonies to past events and as an expressive resource for visual storytelling.

Indeed the indexical character of the photographic image is seen to

Fig. 7. Sean Ó hEochaidh : *The Last Storyteller*

underwrite the documentary film's claim to facticity. The photographic image signals the presence of the camera on the scene at the historical moment of image capture. The archival image appears to be the closest we can get to the original historical reality, a sort of 'second-degree original'.[7] Digitalisation may be changing all this and certainly the expanded opportunities of image manipulation render the evidential status of the photographic image much more problematic. We have long been aware of the possibilities of artifice in photographic practice, in the use of the airbrush and in the cropping of the print, but also in the camera point of view and in the editorial decisions and occlusions of the operator. Digital manipulation – the term is a tautology of course – greatly expands the capacity for departures from the veridical.

So historians beware! With the photographic image all is not always what it seems. We have not only to attend to the *denotative* aspects of the image, what it points to in the world it depicts, but also to its *connotative* elements, its meaning as a cultural statement and its construction as a technological, cultural and representational process.

With this health warning in mind, how should we deal with this stockpile of images that both documentarists and historians pore over and use? Are these to be treated as primary evidence and mute testimony to an unattainable past or as narrative resource capable of releasing the submerged voices of history and of attending to their story?

Over the last number of years, in collaboration with my editors Roger Buck and more recently Simon Hipkins, I have developed an archivally based, creative documentary practice which seeks to explore aspects of Ireland's post-Famine past, including the diaspora. *Hard Road To Klondike / Rotha Mór an tSaoil* (1999) drew on a rich reservoir of early film material, both actuality and fictional in character, in order to retell the classic Irish emigrant story of Mící MacGabhann's tramp through frontier America to the Yukon. *Rebel Frontier* (2004) employed a similar archival strategy, now combined with live action re-enactment, to retell the story of the Irish and Finnish miners of Butte, Montana and their struggle against the Anaconda Copper Company during the First World War. The film, narrated by Martin Sheen, employed the additional device of the 'unreliable narrator'. The story of the momentous events unfolding in Butte is told from the perspective of a Pinkerton agent sent to break the miners' strike. This might be a young Dashiel Hammett. *Child of the Dead End / Tachrán Gan Todhchaí* (2009) deals with the life and work of Donegal-born navvy poet and writer Patrick MacGill. It also employs a rich corpus of archival images alongside dramatic elements somewhat more elaborate than those found in the earlier films.

These films have been heralded for their use of archive, which has been recognised as quite distinctive within documentary film-making in Ireland.[8] More recently, I have been seeking to make sense of my own creative documentary work and its use of archive material as both historical trace and as narrative resource exploited to engage with the past.[9] Hopefully these reflections might illuminate the broader issues around documentary film as historiographical practice raised in the first parts of this paper.

In the article mentioned above, I discuss the sequence in *Klondike* which portrays the arrival of Donegal emigrant Mící Mac Gabhann in New York in the 1890s on board an emigrant ship. This montage involves fictional elements, period actualities of New York (from the Edison paper print collection), short varieties of staged incidents (from the same source) and live-action footage seeking to capture the historical resonances in the contemporary metropolis. As in other found footage films, no attempt is made to discriminate between these different sorts of footage by the use of any framing or titling device (although at one point the soundtrack with its dubbed sound of a cine projector at work does explicitly invite the audience to peep into a 'cinema of attractions'.[10]

The archive material is not used here as it is in many television documentaries to illustrate a didactic argument primarily established via an authoritative voice-over provided by a historian. Stephen Rea voices Mac Gabhann's commentary to provide the film's central narrative thread and does so in an 'actorly' manner. This, I think, lifts the voice to a level of subtlety where voice, image and soundtrack resonate in an evocative manner creating a diegetic space somewhere between fact and fiction.

Nor is the archive material used as evidence of a past 'way of life'. Indeed the use of the archive is on occasions not strictly bound by concerns with complete historical and geographical accuracy (clearly Mac Gabhann's early life was lived before the advent of film and the moving image material assembled to cover this part of his story is from a much later period (much of it from the 1935 film *Aran of the Saints*).

Is the film-maker guilty of playing free and easy with documentary sources? Is he involved in some sleight of hand in this blurring of the boundaries of fact and fiction in the choice of the archival mix?

Fact and Fiction in the Documentary Enterprise

I would see *Klondike* as falling within a tradition of 'found footage' film-making. As Beattie tells us, the found footage or compilation film is one where:

> The found footage film maker may combine nonfictional images selected from sources as varied as commercial stock footage, newsreels, home movies and fiction footage to construct an argument about the socio-historical world.[11]

This sort of film has its origins in a set of avant-garde visual practices based on the found object, the method of collage and on early theories of film montage. Traditional television documentary film-making of course habitually employs elements of the found footage approach, but as Stella Bruzzi notes, it uses archive '. . . illustratively, as part of a historical exposition to complement other elements such as interviews and voice-over'.[12]

In general it does not share the concerns of the found footage film-maker with problematising the sources it uses. Nor is it concerned with making the compilation of the material and its *retournage* an aesthetic end in itself.

The found footage film does not seek to offer the immediate, indexical access to the past promised by the original photographic sources from which it is assembled. In the found footage film the images are all mixed up. Combined together under a montage principle, they establish a different sort of relationship with the past to the indexical claims made for the individual photographic image. The relationship of archival element to historical event becomes a *figurative* rather than a referential one. Found footage film-making lies somewhere between documentary and fictional modes of representation as it does between documentary practice and that of the avant-garde film-maker. It offers a critical reading of history and its sources. As Keith Beattie argues:

Fig. 8. Montage: *Hard Road To Klondike*

In this way, metacommentary and historiography are implicated within a
process in which source or 'found footage' is interrogated via filmic collage
to release functional and valuable ambiguities inherent in the footage.[13]

Thus *The Hard Road To Klondike* seeks to remain faithful to a traditional
practice of storytelling while drawing on the figurative powers of the photographic image and the practices of found footage film-making. The film
recasts the autobiographical recollections of one particular migrant worker
and his passage to the new world. Mící Mac Gabhann's story is a thoroughly
modernist one, speaking as it does to a wider experience of colonised peoples
and of diaspora. This broader theme is explored not only via his account of his
passage to the new world but in his musings on his encounters with the native
American peoples he meets in Montana and later in the Yukon.[14] In turn, our
treatment and its use of found footage casts Mac Gabhann's story in broader
terms. The archival photography employed freed from its indexical 'obligations' can function in a metonymic manner to paint a bigger picture.

Rebel Frontier is also a story of diaspora – in this case the attempt by emigrant Irish and Finnish workers to bring distinctively European traditions of
radicalism (nationalism, socialism and syndicalism) into the US labour movement at a pivotal moment in the class struggle in America. In this case the film
plays the evidential power of the archival image off against the fictive possibilities of the 'unreliable narrator'. In the film we 'embody' the voice-over

(provided by Martin Sheen) in the persona of a Pinkerton agent who identifies himself as 'Abraham Byrne'. Byrne tells us he has been sent to Butte to spy for the Anaconda Copper Company.

ABRAHAM BYRNE (VO)
And who am I you may ask? You can call me Abraham Byrne, in 1917 just twenty-two years old, fresh out of Baltimore and eager for a slice of the action. Up to then my work for the agency had been pretty routine stuff, matrimonial and missing person cases. This I reckoned was gonna be different . . .

He appears fleetingly before the camera as a character throughout the film but his presence is established primarily via his voice-over. The agent looks back over the tumultuous events that took place in Butte and on occasions – such as the lynching of Industrial Workers of the World (IWW) activist Frank Little – is revealed as a possible participant in these events. Dashiell Hammett (1894–1961) had a short career as a Pinkerton agent before emerging as a writer. He appears to have been in Butte, Montana during the labour disturbances that occurred there during the First World War. Later he drew upon this experience in the writing of his classic detective novel *Red Harvest* (1926), also set in Butte, though at a slightly later period. However, in our film the mythic status of Hammett's involvement in the Butte events is identified by a number of interviewees who make clear to us that we may be dealing with rumour, hearsay and legend, in short with the 'contingency of memory', rather than with attested historical fact.

MARK ROSS
Dashiell Hammett came to Butte in 1917 as an operative for the Pinkerton Detective Agency, which had been hired by the Anaconda Company to keep an eye on the miners . . . in the labour unrest that was happening at that time here in town.

DAVE EMMONS
Pinkerton was the favourite agency of the company by that time and amongst the spies who worked here during those years was Dashiell Hammett

KEVIN SHANNON
We know Dashiell Hammett was offered $5,000 . . . you know who Hammett was . . . eh?

JERRY CALVERT
He was employed as a private detective and that formed the basis of his detective fiction later on . . .

Fig. 9. Jacky Corr: *Rebel Frontier*

Our narrator 'Abraham Byrne' can then only be regarded as a potentially unreliable one. He may or may not represent Dashiell Hammett. He may or may not be giving us an accurate account of his activities in Butte. The historical record is unclear and the narration reflects that.

Most of us are aware of the negative portrayal within documentary film criticism of the 'voice of God' narration typically found within much of the documentary output of television. This voice is often didactic in tone, authoritative in manner and expository in form. Voice-over does not have to be like this; it can choose to problematise the historical testimony of its contributors and the truth claims of the documentarist – as in the case of Abraham Byrne in *Rebel Frontier*.

Certainly in all three compilation films discussed here I quite consciously sought to depart from a 'voice of God' narration in favour of a voice-over that had more in common with the 'inner monologue' found in fiction film-making. Here the voice-over is frequently used to reveal a person's inner thoughts and motivations. These can often be ironic and contradictory (although the voice-over can also be asked to provide exposition and narrative coherence). Certainly the impact of using a nuanced voice-over such as that found in *Rebel Frontier* is not only to destablise the veracity of the narration but also to create a different sort of referential relation of voice to archival image to that found in the traditional television documentary.

Child of the Dead End also addresses the problem of evaluating the truth claims of life writing and the veracity of narrations based on such sources. From the beginning in its title sequence it offers the viewer an exploration of 'the fact and fiction of the life of a writer'. Historians have rather assumed that Patrick MacGill's early novels, in particular *Child of the Dead End* (1913) and *The Rat Pit* (1914), can be read as autobiographical accounts of MacGill's time as a navvy in Scotland and accordingly that they are an important historical source for understanding the life of the migrant Irish in pre-First World War Scotland.[15]

I am not sure that is how MacGill saw his work. His first novels combine social documentation and Gothic narrative in equal measure (above all in the tragedy of Norah Ryan, central to each book). I was clear that from the outset our film would have to mirror the ambivalent handling of fact and fiction present in MacGill's work. Accordingly the film archival sequences are segued into dramatic re-enactment of scenes from MacGill's books and vice versa. The original scene from the books may or may not portray events MacGill directly experienced. We simply don't know. Other scenes in the books are clearly fictive in nature and are presented as such in the film. Thus we fairly faithfully follow MacGill's account of the early life of his character Dermod Flynn as a *spalpeen* in Ulster and the west of Scotland provided in *Children of the Dead End*. This element of the book is usually regarded as 'thinly disguised' autobiography, not least because MacGill also rehearses this account in various newspaper interviews he gave. Moreover, his description of the life of the Irish itinerant labourer in Scotland in the first decade of the twentieth century is capable of some degree of verification with regard to the historical record.[16]

The dramatic reconstructions in the film seek congruence with the archival material used, not to try and elide the two and create the illusion of a window on the past but hopefully to open up larger social issues as the drama plays out against a visual record of the time. Why did socialists like MacGill enlist in the

Fig. 10. Dinner Party: *Child of the Dead End*

British Army? How were such men regarded in post-independence Ireland? The interweaving of the two strives to parallel the manner in which fact and fiction, documentary report and Gothic fable mingle in MacGill's life writing, an admixture which proved very successful in helping him achieve realist outcomes as a writer.

Present and past, indexical photographic trace and imaginative re-telling are brought into creative alignment in a manner which hopefully both moves the viewers and causes them to question what they are seeing and what the narrator is telling them. The collision of past and present and of different sorts of documentary images and sounds intermingled with fictive reconstruction provide an interrogation of a key text dealing with Irish migrant experience. The found footage film, like the performative documentary more generally,[17] plots a space between fact and fable. This could be said of most storytelling.

Conclusion

Documentary film-making today is an exciting field of creative innovation where many of the key elements of the practice and their creative use – the archival image, the voice-over, the reconstructed sequence – are currently up for grabs. In reworking these narrational resources as tools for representing and interrogating history, creative documentary film-making is, I believe, doing important historiographical work. Sooner or later history is also going to have to begin to reflect critically on its 'poetics'[18] and its use of narrative, figurative trope and discursive strategy in its practices of writing and conceptualisation. A postmodern history will of necessity also have to reflect on the role of subject position and ideological inflection in the production of the historical text. Such reflections are now commonplace in enlightened documentary film practice.

After all, despite seventy years of social scientific aspiration central to the *Annales* project,[19] history remains what it always has been – an art of telling stories about the past. Perhaps it shares more in common with documentary film-making than it cares to admit.

II
Documentary:
Critical Practice

True North
The ethics of consent

ALAN GILSENAN

A man without ethics is a wild beast loosed upon the world.
Albert Camus, *L'Étranger*[1]

Never before have we been so observed. So recorded. So documented. On every street, in every parking lot, in every shopping centre. Online and elsewhere. In reality and in virtual reality. Each movement. Each transaction. Each encounter. And never before have we documented *ourselves* so much. Recorded our every moment. On our phones, our cameras, our voice-recorders, our social media. We are constantly watching and listening. Ourselves and others. Each and every minute. And we are being watched and listened to. Nearly all of the time.

Yet, in most of these exchanges, our consent is never clearly nor consciously sought. No doubt, there are legal protocols and bureaucratic get-out clauses under-pinning all these transmissions, lost amid the digital small-print, but they remain fundamentally outside of our control. We are all slowly becoming the unknowing subjects in some strange abstract film, an unformed and shapeless documentary of our social netherworld.

In this constantly shifting landscape, the question of consent rarely rises to the forefront of our consciousness. We give it little thought or possibly we just accept it as a fact of life. Some of us, even, are promiscuous in our love affair with ourselves, with our own image, our own fleeting presence on this earth. As if to be seen or heard even momentarily affirms our very existence. Andy Warhol's 'famous for fifteen minutes' theory has become a mere digital blip of ever-after.

In the ghoulish shape of reality television we find the world of an ever-present Big Brotherhood finding its commercial and popular home. In George Orwell's seminal 1949 novel *Nineteen Eighty-Four*, his enigmatic Dictator of Oceania was a figure of all-seeing authoritarianism. For three decades after the novel was published, Big Brother became a by-word for oppressive state control, for the abuse of government power, an anonymous symbol for the erosion of civil liberties. But, in the aftermath of 1984 – the year not the book – we find the rapacious designs of Big Brother are now something to be sought after. We crave his all-seeing eye, now transformed into *our* all-seeing eyes. Big Brother and his bastard sons have metamorphosed into the sweet caress of national television exposure. To be seen. To be heard. To be manipulated. Edited. Exposed. And disposed of, of course. All in the blink of an eye.

For reality television is the wolf-in-sheep's-clothing of the factual television world. Masquerading as documentary, using its grammar and conventions, it proclaims itself as the unbridled truth. TV unplugged. It is, of course, a crude confectionery cooked up and shamelessly manipulated by a huge team of TV executives, executive producers, producers, directors, designers, psychologists, editors and other sundry minions. No doubt, the production teams also boast an expensive array of lawyers who ensure that every participant has signed away their life prior to taking part. The tantalising sniff of possible, albeit fleeting, fame over-rides all other considerations among the carefully chosen and undoubtedly emotionally vulnerable cast.

While consensus is arguably one of the most important pillars of any civilised society, underpinning both our public democracy and our interpersonal relations, it has become an increasingly devalued aspect of documentary production. Yet consensus implies a sort of bland broad-stroke agreement and that, certainly, is not what good documentary should be about. What we are really talking about here, of course, is consent, not consensus: consent is perhaps something nobler. Individual consent seems fundamental to all human relationships, unless, of course, one is a psychopath. (Or possibly a television executive.)

In this world of television, consent equates to a horrible, grubby piece of paper called a 'release form'. This is a sort of intimidating convoluted piece of legal gobbledygook, designed to intimidate participants in any documentary while simultaneously giving great comfort and solace to television company lawyers and high-ranking executives most of whom haven't the faintest clue (nor interest) as to how a documentary is actually made.

Alas, we live in litigious times and the release form serves as a legal contract whereby the participant in any film gives overall rights to the broadcaster or distributor and, while it clearly has a very real role in formalising contractual arrangements, it really has no tangible raison d'être other than 'you don't get bloody sued!' Which, granted, I suppose, is a consideration.

But the reality of making any documentary is fundamentally about building trust with complete strangers, and establishing that trust is a very delicate, time-consuming and highly personal business. Now trust is not exactly easy to legislate for. It is far more of a subtle art than an exact science. But it is, nonetheless, the guiding principle which underpins all documentary making. So, naturally, after possibly months of building that trust, the prospect of waving a release form beneath the nose of your participant does not fill any film-maker with joy. Firstly, it seems somewhat crass, as if all previous discussions were just a meaningless courtship and now one is crudely moving in for the kill. Secondly, even a signed release form carries little moral weight if the participant ultimately feels shafted by the finished film (except, of course, for the gleeful executive gibbering all the way to the steps of the courthouse). Thirdly, and most importantly, the release form divests all power from the subject of the film. It removes their rights while failing to acknowledge that the producers of the film in question have any obligations whatsoever to the person or subject contributing to the production.

So while legal consent is one thing, moral consent remains another. But, as we found while making a number of documentary series set in Irish institutions, moral consent is very complicated to obtain. While filming *The Asylum* (2005), a four-part documentary series for Radio Telefís Éireann (RTÉ) about St Ita's psychiatric hospital in Portrane, north Co. Dublin, we encountered a wide array of moral dilemmas.[2] Some were very straightforward such as in the case of 'George' (not his real name). George was the first person I met when I first came to visit the hospital. He was a Beckettian figure about the corridors, complete with stylish hat and dark overcoat. He paced the lengthy haunted corridors endlessly, although not with the anxious gait of some of the others. He had a certain air of dignity, perhaps even demonstrating in some way how he was quietly above it all. He had lived at St Ita's for over fifty years and was now, as the uncrowned king of lunatics, a benign presence about the place although the older staff remember him being difficult. Like us all, George had mellowed with age.

Fig. 11. *The Asylum*

We had many chats, smoked many Sweet Aftons and filmed extensively with him. He seemed to enjoy it all, relished the attention perhaps. For George was one of our stars, an old-style leading man. But I had always said – as I always do – that he could pull out at any point up until late in the editing. This is, admittedly, a slightly high-risk strategy and flies somewhat in the face of conventional wisdom. But it seems to work. It gives people the confidence to get started. The sense of not being under undue pressure and that there is an escape hatch. So that is always the deal. Respect the autonomy of each person and allow them to change their minds – even at the last moment – as some did.

George was among them. One bright Saturday morning, close to the broadcast, I went out to visit Portrane. George hadn't been well lately and so I dropped into Unit 9 to see him. He said, simply and quite out of the blue, that he thought he didn't really want to be in the film. Taken slightly aback, I checked again. 'Yes, I'm not sure I want to be seen on the television as a class of madman,' he replied, 'but I enjoyed all our chats, I really did'. I said that I understood and that it was fine. When I mentioned it to staff, they thought he was just out-of-sorts and that he'd come around. But he didn't. So we took him out.

Shortly after, and quite suddenly, George died. A distant but kindly sister emerged from Canada. It would, she felt, be a lovely tribute to George to include him in the film. The staff agreed. We could put him back in and she would sign the release form. (No problem there for the steely TV executives.) But we didn't. George had said no and that was that. Man-to-man, spit-in-the-palm, no lawyers need apply.

But I still miss George from *The Asylum*. I miss his stories of life as a merchant seaman, of adventures on the Canadian plains. I miss his roguish romancing, his wry humour, his insightful moments, his disturbing memories of strait-jackets: 'Houdini would have just gone "whoosh" and he'd be free.' Arrogantly perhaps, I regret that his life will have gone undocumented like so many before him in the Irish mental health service. Like the thousands who lie in unmarked graves in the Portrane graveyard overlooking the sea. But no doubt he is happier his way. No doubt, now gone to his eternal rest, his elegant if troubled spirit will live on in the memories of other patients who knew him, and in the affections of those who cared so well for him. And in our memories too.

So George was straightforward. No moral difficulties there. Deal done. But with others, it was not so simple. Earlier on in the production process, we had discussed the whole notion of ethical consent with the clinical director of St Ita's, the softly spoken but inspiring figure of Dr Richard Blennerhassett. He quietly reminded us that we must always remember to firstly respect the autonomy of the patients. ('Clients' is probably the correct term but it always seemed so dispassionate and uncaring to me.) After that, we agreed that we would consult with the relevant family members or loved one as well as consulting the appropriate psychiatric staff. So that was that, our triple-lock system of consent: patient, family, staff. Foolproof, or so we hoped.

Another part of our early discussions was that I assured Dr Blennerhassett that should he – for any reason – decide, in his clinical opinion, that it was not in the best interests of any patient to be part of the film that I would remove them from the documentary. No questions asked. It was a sort of gentleman's agreement, I liked to think. This, too, was perhaps a risky strategy, seemingly relinquishing a certain amount of editorial control, but I liked and trusted the director. I felt that he understood what we were trying to achieve. But also we drew comfort and reassurance from the fact that he – not I – was making the professional judgement on the mental health of our beloved residents and participants. Thankfully, he never had to make that particular call but I was glad that we had agreed on it all the same. (Oh, and no lawyers were involved here either.)

From Fred Wiseman's *Titicut Follies* (1967) to Milos Foreman's *One Flew Over The Cuckoo's Nest* (1975), film-makers adore making films about the insane. It appeals both to their sense of themselves but also to their sense of the theatrical. And there was a patient in the Acute Unit at St Ita's who was the film-maker's dream. 'Frank' was your stereotypical madman and therefore a joy to behold. Straight out of central casting, most of the time Frank believed he was Elvis Presley. (Dumb question from film-maker: 'So when did you start to like Elvis?' Frank's reply: 'Like Elvis? I *am* Elvis. Do I like myself might be a better question.' Fair point.) On occasion, Frank also believed himself to be Jesus Christ but mainly he was Elvis. In the green neon-lit corridors, as soon as the cameras rolled, he would give us passable renditions of 'Blue Suede Shoes' and 'Don't Be Cruel'. We loved him and he, it appeared, seemed to love us. But he also had a strangely perceptive understanding of his own mental condition, and his boundless energy and happy spirit were, at times, the perfect antidote to the darkness and distress that one encountered in the Acute Unit.

So we went to consult with Frank's family. We understood that they might have reservations about it all. There was a large family meeting, a lengthy and open discussion. They understood what we were trying to achieve and they accepted that our motives were solid enough. And that Frank was very happy. And that he was enjoying the filming. 'But, it's just . . . it's just . . . well . . . what would the neighbours think? How would the children feel if other kids in the playground started saying "we saw your uncle on the telly last night and he's a total maddser! Loo-la! Nut-bag!"?'

Which was all very understandable, of course. But what of Frank's autonomy? Of respecting him despite his mental illness? And was that not the point of the series: let's not hide the mentally ill away like they are freaks, untouchables, never to be accepted or discussed or acknowledged. Or are we – the film-makers – the ones that are actually complicit in the freak show? Did we not enjoy Frank's caricatured madman performance? Did he not bestow a sort of dramatic shimmer on our dull documentary portrait? Are both we and his family only satisfying our own selfish needs?

To this day, I'm not sure of the answer. But we left Frank out of the films, just to be safe. To be fair to his family. To respect their wishes. But, somehow, I still have a lingering concern that conservatism won out in the end. That Frank had been silenced. That Elvis had left the building. As if he had never been there at all. Sometimes consent is hard to achieve. But not always.

For lastly, there was Angus. A solicitor by profession, Angus suffered with bi-polar depression. He was living mainly in what we quaintly term 'in the community', in other words, on the outside, although real 'community' seems hard to come by these days in Dublin. We had talked to him and filmed him attending the day clinic in the suburb of Artane. He spoke openly and honestly about his highs and lows – his highs mainly. But he felt that, in order to get a true picture of his life, we needed to film him in his 'high' state. We discussed this at length and decided that we would film him – if and when it occurred – and then we could discuss whether to broadcast it later when he 'comes down to earth' again.

Some months later, Angus was committed to the Acute Unit. We arrived to film and met with him in the dayroom. With some hesitation and considerable unease, we began to film. Dressed in pyjamas and dressing gown, he strode about the room, reminding me strangely of the stern father in the film *Mary Poppins* (1964), Mr Banks, who slightly loses the plot towards the end. Raving. 'Let's go fly a kite . . . up to the highest height.' Not all complete nonsense either. Excited talk of reforming the legal system. The Canadian model was interesting. Despite my disquiet, I admired his energy and passion.

A sharp knock on the door from a senior nurse terminated the interview abruptly and against Angus's wishes. She was unaware of our arrangement and the prior agreement with his clinical team. But you could hardly question her natural instinct to protect a vulnerable patient. We were happy to respect her judgement but concerned about whether we were equally respecting Angus's autonomy and his right to speak – even though he was clearly not himself as we knew him and was also heavily medicated.

Some weeks later, when Angus had 'come back to himself' again, we met up with him to show him the footage. It was uncomfortable viewing for all but he felt happy with it and happy that it would contribute to the wider understanding of mental illness. (We also filmed Angus watching the footage because we felt that the audience would wish to see that he had been included in the process of deciding whether or not to incorporate it into the film.)

Angus did give his consent and was very courageous to do so, for in many respects he was opening himself to scrutiny and possibly even to ignominy. But on the morning following the broadcast, he walked out of his home and stood at a nearby bus stop. In the grey early morning light, there was only one other man waiting with him. After a few moments, the man turned and reached out his hand: 'I saw you on the television last night and I just wanted to say well done. It was a brave thing to do.' It reflected the common response that all the participants in this and other documentaries were greeted with. Sometimes, it seems, simple truth and honesty has its rewards.

Consent is clearly difficult to achieve. But it remains a worthy aspiration, despite the increasing pressures to side-step it. Consent is messy, a pain in the ass that gets in the way of a good story. It involves talk and understanding and compromise. And these things take time. 'Oh, just get them to sign the bloody release and be damned . . . aren't they lucky to be on television at all?' In Ireland, increasing competition between the public service broadcaster RTÉ and a flourishing array of independent, digital and satellite stations has led to an over-emphasis on things such as 'market share' and 'audience reach'. The cinema has fared little better. In this ferocious marketplace, producers are under increased pressure to mould the truth into a more dramatic storyline or, as Tony Blair might have it, to 'sex it up'. Most stories are now told in the loud shouty language of tabloid journalism. Every minor revelation is an extraordinary exposé, every misjudgement a shocking scandal. And all this in starkly contrasting black and white. No shades of grey, no subtle gradations and no moral complications are allowed in this soap opera landscape of half-light, half-truths and hype. And all this with a grand air of self-congratulation.

But does all this talk of consent and ethical considerations begin to sound both antiquated and high-minded? Do these noble notions appeal, somehow, to our sense of self-importance, to the natural egotism of documentary makers? To our 'truth-telling' complex, our holier-than-thou attitudes, our faux sincerity? For we are, of course, skilled manipulators and professional snake-charmers, as well as earnest campaigners and miners for truth.

So today, are ethics relevant, or even necessary, in this non-ideological and cynical age? Is there a need for a guiding code of practice? A 'best practice scenario', to coin a phrase that itself speaks of blandness and lack of imagination. Interestingly, there have been some recent attempts to formulate ethical models for documentary. The Center for Social Media at the American University in Washington DC conducted a study of forty-five US film-makers and their approach to ethics.[3] The incisive report reflects the uncertainty of the whole endeavour. It concludes:

> When filmmakers face ethical conflicts, they often resolve them in an ad-hoc way, keeping their deep face-to-face relationship with subjects and their more abstract relationship with the viewers in balance with practical concerns about cost, time, and ease of production.
>
> The ethical conflicts put in motion by these features of a filmmaker's embattled-truth-teller identity are, ironically for a truth-telling community,

unable to be widely shared or even publicly discussed in most individual cases. Sometimes filmmakers are constrained by contract, but far more often they are constrained by the fear that openly discussing ethical issues will expose them to risk of censure or may jeopardise the next job.

Filmmakers thus find themselves without community norms or standards. Institutional standards and practices remain proprietary to the companies for which the filmmakers may be working and do not always reflect the terms they believe are appropriate to their craft. Their communities are far-flung, virtual, and sporadically rallied at film festivals and on listservs. Filmmakers need to share both experience and vocabulary and to be able to question their own and others' decision-making processes without encountering prohibitive risk.

One inherent difficulty with documentary is that it is a very fluid and uncertain discipline. One aspect to this lack of clarity is that the term 'documentary' can straddle both the worlds of art and journalism. In the arts, of course, there is no place for morality or ethics of any kind. But journalism? Even someone as wonderfully contrary as Oscar Wilde agreed that there should be ethics in journalism (particularly with regard to himself) while art was no place for the leaden world of social responsibility and grimy reality:

> No great artist ever sees things as they really are. If he did, he would cease to be an artist.[4]

In the end, the simple truth is that truth is never simple. In the words of Oscar Wilde:

> The truth is rarely pure and never simple. Modern life would be very tedious if it were either.[5]

Life – and its reflected image that is the uncertain world of smoke and mirrors of documentary film-making – is complex and complicated. In this uncertain environment, it is hugely difficult to legislate for right and wrong, and one can only follow one's own lights, one's own moral compass, one's own true north. In the end, ethics is fundamentally about honesty and respect for others, and ethics for documentary making are no different. I appreciate that I may seem a little old-fashioned in all this. My father too was an old-fashioned man and he was fond of old-fashioned phrases. Two particular favourites of his were 'common decency' and 'common courtesy'. Now common decency and common courtesy can be applied to many things, large and small. They speak of community and shared values, of a certain democratic spirit. They speak too of traditions handed down, of understood moral truths. Of respect for each other.

Common decency. Common courtesy. In all matters, large and small.

The quotation from Camus' *L'Étranger* at the opening of this piece was recently appropriated by the website of an American right-wing Christian organisation. The sheer absurdity of this would surely have provoked a wry smile from the great French-Algerian author. It proves how utterly subjective, how gloriously ambiguous all this talk of ethics really is and that the very notion of a definite set of documentary ethics remains as elusive as ever.

But then, as Albert Camus also wrote in his 1942 philosophical treatise *The Myth of Sisyphus*: 'Integrity has no need of rules.'[6]

The Power of One
Dear Daughter and
Stolen Lives

LOUIS LENTIN

Consider the chain of events. If in 1992, Christine Buckley had *not* told her story on RTÉ Radio 1 to Gay Byrne. Most likely I would have paid the programme scant attention and in all probability not have made *Dear Daughter* (1996). Our national broadcaster might not have followed with *States of Fear*. There would have been no apology on behalf of the state from the then taoiseach Bertie Ahern, no Child Abuse Commission, no Redress Board, no Ryan Report. The many survivors of rampant industrial school abuse would have been left to suffer on silently. All it needed was the 'power of one' to start the chain reaction and for the horrors to be exposed. Others had spoken out, notably Paddy Doyle in 1989 in his terrifying testament *The God Squad* but despite a 'Person of the Year Award for an Outstanding Contribution to Irish Society', the essence of Paddy's contribution was ignored. The man in the street who claimed to know it all and in reality knew nothing didn't want to know. My own attempt within RTÉ to tell Paddy's story on film, seventeen years prior to *Dear Daughter*, was resolutely brushed under the carpet as 'too harrowing'.

But Christine did speak out. The public did react, many with disbelief or outright rejection, but many sought her help. I too sought her out to propose that Crescendo Concepts produce a documentary film to be submitted to RTÉ, telling her story and of related events during her thirteen years in St Vincent's industrial school, Dublin, run by the Sisters of Mercy, known simply as Goldenbridge. After some consideration Ms Buckley agreed to my proposal. I had gained, if not her full trust, enough to allow us both to move forward. But first I needed to know the full story, in detail. I listened with increasing shock as it all flowed out, Christine hop-skipping from one experience to the other, seemingly remembering everything in detail. I became immersed in the morass of abuse that formed not only her childhood life but also that of many others. Given such emotional material there was a limit as to how often it could be recounted. Accordingly, we agreed to proceed for an hour or two, one night a week over the next few weeks, each session designed not only to progress the story but to deal with it, section by section in detail. Accordingly, over six weekly recorded sessions, apart from

66

Fig. 12. Christina Buckley, from opening sequence of *Dear Daughter*

an occasional interjection, Christine poured her heart out. What evolved was
the story of a search:

> I wanted to find my parents and kill them for every ounce of pain that I suf-
> fered because of what they did. I wanted to find my Dad and say: 'I'm
> suffering because of you . . . and the likes of you.'

Born in 1946 of an affair between a married Dublin woman, separated from
her husband, and a Nigerian medical student who refused to accept the child, she
was given up by her mother at three weeks and placed in Temple Hill orphanage,
eventually to be deposited without explanation by her third foster parent in
Goldenbridge:

> I was four years and two months when I went to Goldenbridge orphanage .
> . . It was the 22nd of December 1950. It was hell . . . absolutely sheer hell.
> Kids didn't look like humans . . . they looked like animals. You were
> constantly beaten, flogged for nothing. All I remember is screaming,
> screaming, screaming . . . kids being beaten, beaten, beaten.

Some forty years later, lying in hospital with cervical cancer she reflected on the possibility of dying without knowing anything of her parents. On discharge, she set about finding them. Constantly discouraged and thwarted by various officials, she fought on, as Christine does, eventually meeting her mother in Dublin and tracking down her father, by then a successful doctor in Nigeria. After numerous letters he eventually replied: 'Dear Daughter . . .'

I had a title, but how to shape this shattering material for television, how best to tell it and fund it was the challenge. Prompted by the strength and detail with which Christine spoke, for a time I mulled over the idea of having her tell her own story alone, direct to camera with minimal intervention over six recorded half-hours to be transmitted nightly throughout one week. I alerted the commissioning editor of RTÉ's Independent Production Unit, to the project before the annual submission date for independent productions, mentioning the 'streaming' approach. A non-starter; I should have known RTÉ would never countenance clearing six half-hour prime slots for a whole week. What I eventually submitted, with two pages of story outline, was:

> Dear Daughter . . . will not be a cosy reunion between parents and daughter. Rather it will allow Christine to confront both her parents with the hell she went through because of them, as well as confronting those nuns involved from Goldenbridge . . . plus others who hindered her search. Visual and sound images will recreate events from the orphanage, Christine's search for and eventual meeting with her mother in Dublin and her father in Nigeria.

In hindsight, a little vague. I had no idea who might agree to be involved. However, the following correspondence ensued:

> 24 November 1993
> Thank you for submitting your proposal, *Dear Daughter* . . . for consideration as a single documentary in 1994 . . . your proposal is now on [that] short list.

> 30 May 1994
> We have now considered our decision-making for 1994 and regrettably your proposal was not among those commissioned . . . I would however, welcome the opportunity to consider the proposal in 1995.
> (Commissioning Editor, Independent Productions)

It seemed crazy that RTÉ couldn't immediately see the wider social implications of this story. However, with fingers crossed that their 'consideration' in 1995 would be positive, I ploughed on. From the outset it was obvious that every aspect of the wider story had to be researched in detail. To gain the full trust of those I spoke with, I felt it vital that I research everything personally, talk to everybody, meeting with as many as possible myself, initially from a small number of 'Goldenbridge girls' with whom Christine had stayed in touch, most in Ireland, some in England.

The risk of exposing her on her own was more than obvious. There was no question of doubt or disbelief, but for Christine's own sake, for the sake of so many, as producer I had to be able to stand over everything; everything had to be verified, supported and fully backed up. There was no doubt in my mind that once we transmitted all would be questioned, cross-examined, picked at; as indeed it was.

And so we met, one at a time, spoke for hours by phone or communicated by letter, each woman telling me, giving her story, willingly – pleased at last to have someone prepared to listen. Each contact leading to others. I became a listening forum, the phone constantly ringing with someone *needing* to talk, to tell, to share. Overall, I must have gathered at least fifty accounts of the hell of childhood under the 'care' of the Sisters of Mercy at Goldenbridge during Christine's years there. 'Sisters of Mercy,' the girls would softly sing, 'have mercy on us.' Yes, there were a few who spoke warmly of the nuns and would have nothing to do with the film. But as time and talk proceeded it became crystal clear that the overwhelming majority lived with an ingrained memory of years of physical and mental abuse, beatings, degradation, starvation, humiliation, to whom recall was not a problem.

In parallel, hours were spent going over and over the smallest detail with Christine: events, addresses, places, times, names. She never varied. Everything then was verified and checked with girls who had witnessed or experienced the same and remembered. Anybody I could trace, and who was involved, was sought: 'care workers', girls who had grown up in and had remained in Goldenbridge (regarded by some of the children as more cruel than the nuns), all of whom refused to talk; Mammy Martin who, with her husband Daddy Martin, despite a small house full of their own children, had befriended and sought to adopt her, only to be refused by the Mercy nuns; the Sister in Charge of the adoption agency who eventually, under pressure, arranged Chris's initial meeting with her mother; lay teachers from Goldenbridge. In addition, medical records from the Mercy Order and local hospitals particularly Dr Steevens' hospital and St Michael's in Phoenix Park were chased but in vain, nothing it seems had survived. Goldenbridge's own records conveniently burned in a fire.

August 1994 saw *Dear Daughter* again submitted to RTÉ with a short VHS 'to introduce you to Christine and brief extracts from her life'.

3 November 1994

Dear Louis,
Thank you for submitting your proposal *Dear Daughter* for possible commission . . . I am happy to tell you that RTÉ is interested in principle in funding the proposal . . .

(Commissioning Editor)

In May 1995, roughly two years from first submission, the vital contract with RTÉ was finally signed. The Irish Film Board (IFB) had previously come 'on side' with production funding. Granada was showing interest, as were Cori International London, as distributors. However, despite my efforts to persuade them that *Dear Daughter* would undoubtedly attract a large emigrant Irish audience, many of whom had survived the horrors of Irish industrial schools, both eventually opted out, as did three other British broadcasters. Naturally, my hope was that, given the essential involvement of the home broadcaster, a UK company could be convinced to join in. As I pointed out, many of those who had lived through Irish industrial schools now lived in the UK. A trans-mission agreement or co-production involvement would have provided for additional production finance, apart from attracting *that* large Irish audience.

After a lot of thought and consideration of style, form, shape, visual and sound treatment, I arrived at a format and loose shooting script that broke nat-urally into two parts: I: 'childhood and Goldenbridge'; II: 'the story of the search'. It involved recreating as much as possible the significant events; at times with Christine on her own, others with the women who as young girls had experienced and remembered; others, where necessary, with actors at times visually relating one to the other. Apart from the few lines of narration, nothing would be scripted. The 'girls' and Christine would tell it in their own words.

The classic approach to film documentary, rightly, has always been the truth, the whole truth and nothing but the truth, actors recreating sequences being viewed with suspicion. However, holding to my long-held belief in Grierson's classic definition of documentary film as 'the creative treatment of actuality',[1] if actors provided the only way to portray essential events, then I saw no reason why not. It is vital that a documentary film be as finely cast as the best feature. Not only the actors, but all the *real* participants must be able to deliver, to relate on camera what they know in a manner that is absolutely believable, clear and forthright. From among the many I met and had spoken with, I finally asked – and cast – perhaps six former 'Goldenbridge girls', first explaining to each what I would be asking of them on camera. All willingly agreed to participate in what, I warned, could turn out to be an extremely painful experience.

We were moving on, locations sought and found, all twenty eight roles cast, including three wonderful girls to portray Christine at four, in her early teens and at sixteen. Obviously it was essential that I contact the Sisters of Mercy, inform them of our intentions and obtain what co-operation I could. Having viewed the front of Goldenbridge – the iron gate, the long pathway to the front door – it was imperative for the sake of exactitude that I film there; there could be no alternative. Any other location, no matter how similar, could and would be identified as fake. Initial contact was made in mid-July 1995 by phone with Sr Helena O'Donoghue, then provincial leader in charge of the school, followed by a letter outlining the film's intent and requesting a meeting. We met informally and pleasantly in the National Concert hall café, to be exact, when I conveyed what I knew of pertinent events in Goldenbridge and my plan for *Dear Daughter*. Our agreed agenda listed permission to film in the approach grounds, interior hallway, the possible use of one or two classrooms and a large staircase with a landing. We also requested Sr O'Donoghue's participation and, to my mind more importantly, an interview with or involvement by Sr Xaveria, the sister in charge of Goldenbridge during Christine's time, along with Sr Fabian who succeeded her, a year or so before Chris left. Permission was granted by letter from Sr O'Donoghue 'to film in the grounds from gate to convent door and convent hallway'; participation by Sr Helena to be 'confined to an interview'; but Srs Xaveria and Fabian 'will not be interviewed and their names may not be mentioned or stated in the programme in any way whatsoever'.[2]

While pressing again for Sr Xaveria's participation, having got the essential frontage, I had no alternative but to accept the strictures. However, had the Sisters of Mercy allowed participation by Sr Xaveria, it is likely that *Dear Daughter* would have been quite a different film. On the whole the order was co-operative, providing rooms both sides of the hallway for make-up and wardrobe, but keeping a wary eye on us throughout the shoot.

Productions rarely proceed through the pre-production stage in an orderly fashion. Despite RTÉ's financial input (their standard figure for a one-hour documentary at the time) plus the loan agreement from the IFB, and despite some 'crew and facility deals', our 'bare bones budget' still fell well short of the bottom line. Calling for twenty-eight actors, make-up, wardrobe, design, apart from crew, original music, post-production, etc., the production could not be achieved within the normal funding available. Indeed, the lack of a 'development line' in RTÉ's 1995 Budget Summary Form meant my two years' work to date became another 'deferred payment', a not unusual 'never never' item accepted in the hope that additional work be available to keep going. Thankfully, in 1993 when I embarked with Christine, Crescendo Concepts was busy completing *The Quality of Rapture*, a profile on Irish soprano Regina Nathan, and starting production on the second season of *McKenna's Ireland*.

Despite, however, an increase from the Film Board, the financial shortfall was still too large for comfort. Thankfully, during a casual conversation, James Flynn, then IFB's business manager, suggested I contact Eugene Fanning at Arthur Cox solicitors and elicit his help to apply for Section 35 funding, the government's tax-break scheme which I had assumed applied only to features. Under Eugene's friendly guidance, endless meetings, even more endless form filling, and the creation of a dedicated production company, Sablegrange Ltd., the production with the smallest budget hitherto to approach the Department of Arts Culture and the Gaeltacht acquired a Section 35 licence that enabled us to just about bridge the gap.

In the middle of all this, anxious to keep the impetus moving, I decided to make a start and get as much as possible of Christine's to-camera sequences on tape. Within a few hours, on one summer afternoon in lighting cameraman Peter Dorney's living room, all were 'in the can'. Those 'takes' form the spine of the film. Twelve days of principal photography was held until one weekend in mid-October, when Anne Armstrong, Bernadette Fahy, Caroline Hunt, Julia Cooney, Kathleen O'Neill, Sheila Doyle and Chris gathered in what they enthused was the perfect location, with the appearance and creepy feel of the real thing. Here they recreated as many of their memories of Goldenbridge as we could realistically film, starting with each in turn stating their number – 'some of the little kids had to learn off their name because you had a number.' Over an intense two days they re-experienced what you see in the film, mostly in one take. How they got through what I asked for, I will never know. My concern that they might not remember how to string rosary beads, for example, was needless; as soon as they saw the beads and the wire, they started. Everything from their childhood had obviously been 'burnt in'.

Only four sequences didn't make the final cut, entirely due to my failure to find a means of making them convincing: Anne Armstrong reliving how, when thirsty at night, she and the other youngsters had no option but to scoop and drink water from the foul toilets; a small child placed in a large tumble drier and spun once or twice (one doll); Christine and another young girl tied by their ankles to door knobs, one each side of a large door, then swiftly swung backwards and forwards (two dolls) and finally a sequence showing how as children they had to pluck and gather long grass on their knees.

One of the final sequences recorded was my interview with Sr Helena O'Donoghue. Obviously, she had no personal involvement in the events of over thirty years previous but now, however, as current Provincial in Charge, she was having to 'take the rap'. I was fully conscious that the facts I was laying before her and seeking a response to were deeply wounding to her and the order to whom she had committed her life. I had no desire to hurt; nevertheless, there were questions to be put and answers given. At one point, a 'break' became essential. At the end of the session we *both* emerged shattered.

My usual practice before starting to edit is to review all time-coded takes on VHS, finishing with a paper edit listing of the best. Christine, despite an open door into the following four weeks' edit, preferred to wait until we had a final cut which she then viewed through tears. There was no way that any film concerning her life, and that of the many at Goldenbridge, could completely encompass all its horrors as she would have wished. Editor Jörgen Andréason and I both agreed we had the balance right and were gratified that RTÉ and the IFB accepted the cut without changes. Once RTÉ had the tapes, news started to reach us of assistant commissioning editors and others viewing in tears. I knew we had achieved something terrifically strong that would be sensationally effective. Little did I know to what extent!

Once publicity for *Dear Daughter* started the weekend before transmission on Thursday 22 February on RTÉ 1, with Sr Xaviera's identity exposed by the press, reference to child abuse, Goldenbridge, and the role of the nuns was rarely out of the media. Before, and more so following transmission, it became *the* social issue, evoking intense public debate, editorials and letters to the editor, reports of Garda and health board investigations and enquiries. Almost every journalist in the country had something to say on the matter, either for or against, downright sceptical or supportive: 'The feelings of outrage that the film stirred were immediately tempered by feelings of guilt and shame and complicity – feelings that were reinforced with every passing day as revelation followed revelation . . .'[3] Over that first weekend and days prior to the showing, Christine and I seemed to be on every radio programme possible, aspects of the film questioned and answered so often that I feared a danger of pre-empting our potential audience. I needn't have worried. Almost 950,000 people, a third of viewers throughout the country, watched the programme, gaining RTÉ its largest rating for any documentary either before or since. Our phones never stopped, so many stories, so many expressing an urgency to be heard, so many who had never before ventured to speak found themselves with voice. Too many were anonymous anti-Semitic voices which my wife Ronit fielded, personal accusations of church bashing, but also many letters of support. Support not matched by the several TDs and senators contacted who, promising to raise our plea for a government enquiry in the Dáil and Senate, never once opened their mouths.

Prior to transmission, the congregation of the Sisters of Mercy, apologising for the personal hurt and distress caused to children over thirty years ago, expressing 'the deepest regret and sorrow', established a confidential helpline open to callers immediately following the broadcast. Despite that apology, so much ongoing suffering could have been avoided had they not waited thirteen years before the Ryan Report revealed that the Sisters of Mercy were aware of the events documented by *Dear Daughter* before it was aired. When it was being made, the congregation commissioned Mr Gerard Crowley, a childcare specialist, to carry out an investigation into Goldenbridge industrial school (in which I briefly participated) in an effort to provide the congregation with an independent view of what happened there, and to give the congregation some assistance in deciding how to respond to the allegations that were being made. For present purposes, it is sufficient to note that it reached a preliminary view that the allegations were broadly credible.[4]

What ensued, and of primary importance was that now, to a far greater extent than hitherto, those who had suffered abuse such as the film exposed were for the first time being believed. That is until RTÉ did the unbelievable, when on 23 April *Prime Time* aired with a programme featuring an interview with Sr Xaveria that I can only describe as damage limitation.[5] Christine and I had heard of the programme during its making. Its interviewer, Ursula Halligan, returning my call, assured me that Christine and I would both be involved. Christine was interviewed, but I never heard from Ms Halligan again. Until revealed and promo'd on *The Late Late Show*, only a few people, seemingly sworn to secrecy, knew that they had scooped an interview with Sr Xaveria. I watched the programme, which had all the hallmarks and appearance of a PR exercise, with disbelief as implications of 'false memory' were touted against the girls from Goldenbridge, but not of the good sister who throughout was treated with kid-glove deference as a kindly frail old lady, humbly apologising for any 'unintentional hurt she caused'. Never before or since has a broadcaster been known to cast such serious doubts on a major production that it itself had commissioned. The damage had been done. All belief and credibility the survivors of abuse had gained was now once again in tatters. Not to believe was again to betray the many already betrayed.

Sunday prior to that edition of *Prime Time*, Just One Happy Day, an event organised by Christine no doubt with the help of her supportive family, took place at the Royal Dublin Society; a joyous gathering of over five hundred men and women, mostly women, who had lived their childhood in Irish industrial schools and orphanages. The inimitable Ms Buckley had issued a public appeal for donations of teddy bears and other small soft cuddly toys denied to them as institutionalised children; now there was one for everybody. During those few happy hours I, however, found myself approached by men who as boys had been in industrial schools, each wanting me to tell their story. We found a relatively quiet corner and I listened as each told of rampant cruelty, of physical, psychological and endemic sexual abuse. All I could promise was that I would try.

Preliminary research provided enough information for me to submit a strongly worded proposal to RTÉ under the title *Our Boys' Stories* only to have it dismissed by the head of Independent Production with the glib remark: 'Sure everybody knows about this.' No, I pointed out, they did not! I was talking about sexual abuse. Yes, people suspected it went on, but they didn't know the details, and details matter.

Some short time later I received a courtesy call from Mary Raftery, then an RTÉ producer, telling me that she would be producing a three-part series that aimed to examine and expose abuse throughout the wide range of Ireland's industrial schools and institutions. I offered any assistance I could. That series, *States of Fear*, when shown in 1999 rightly and effectively provoked an unprecedented response leading to an apology on behalf of the state by the Taoiseach, the establishment of the Commission on Child Abuse and all that was to follow. Ten years later the publication of the Ryan Report vindicated those of us who had made *Dear Daughter* instrumental in opening up the issue of abuse suffered by children 'in care'.

For a long time following that seminal film, letters continued to arrive from women and men who had suffered similar if not worse abuse in so many industrial schools and institutions. All wrote of its effect on their lives, of addiction, drugs, drink, violence, murder, early death, shame, isolation, loneliness, multiple suicide attempts and inability to form relationships. Arising from those letters and calls, it was obvious that the whole story had yet to be told; the ongoing effect of the myriad forms of abuse, sexual and otherwise, of both girls and boys, as yet unmentioned:

> I never had a life . . .; When I left I was handed a paper bag . . .; I couldn't read or write . . .; They took my life away from me . . .; I never stood a chance . . .; I didn't belong in this 'world'. . .

As one man described his departure from Artane:

> I was leaving Artane . . . he turned to us, his face purple with rage. He said 'So you think you are great going out to the outside world . . . but let me tell you this, very few of you will get on. Most of you will end up in mental homes and prisons . . . some of you will even be hung . . .' Right now I could name six Artane men serving life in England.

Having been rebuffed by RTÉ, I approached TV3 with a programme idea under the heading *Stolen Lives* (1999) to be:

> . . . driven by an examination of 'cause and effect', the result of institutionalisation which for too many years has effected almost 150,000 Irish citizens, many of whom have left the country with no wish ever to return . . .

TV3 responded positively on proviso that the Irish Film Board agree to a matching 50 per cent of the minuscule budget, which they did. The final 48-minute programme, for transmission within TV3's current affairs programme *20/20*, would be cognisant of current developments, i.e. the Taoiseach's apology and the establishment of the Commission on Child Abuse.

Within a short time so much vivid material was recorded, more than enough for three films which TV3 and the Irish Film Board agreed to accept for the price of one. The first, *Our Boys' Stories*, centring on men, also invited a former young Christian Brothers postulant to recount 'the process of initiation' to a world in which boys from a very young age were encouraged to believe that they were above the law, answerable only to their superiors: 'If you didn't buck the system a life on the missions awaited, transgress and Artane or Letterfrack loomed.' The second, *We Were only Children*, related the experiences of four women, two from Goldenbridge and two from St Anne's, Booterstown, in which, to quote journalist Liam Fay, 'the pain and the fury of these women is at times almost unbearable, but it is the tales they tell that will make you want to look away.'[6] The third film was a singularly shocking story not only of deprivation, physical and psychological, but also of extreme and continuous sexual abuse on a young girl of ten, also in St Anne's.

After airing *Our Boys' Story* in October 1999, TV3 chose not to transmit the programmes consecutively as intended, holding *We Were only Children* until the following January and bowing to legal advice not to show the third, *Philomena's Story*, at all. Despite my protests, for a time it appeared it would never be seen. Eventually the decision was taken to broadcast all three, each with an introduction by the eminent psychiatrist and broadcaster the late Professor Anthony Clare expressing his absolute belief in their content. Despite strong, relentless and persistent church opposition, *Philomena's Story* was eventually aired in November 2000 following which Professor Clare, under pressure, decided to remove his affirmation.

Dear Daughter and *Stolen Lives* were undoubtedly milestones in my life that took their toll. I cannot but commit to work in hand, once eliciting a friendly warning that I should avoid being 'too passionate'. I know what was meant, but it is a factor over which I, and others who may likewise be guilty, succumb. All productions absorb fully; what's wrong with a little passion? Involve yourself for years in the above two programmes and emotions are rarely far from the surface. At least, I cannot make such programmes and walk away from them. But the time comes when, if you are to retain your objectivity, your judgement and remain in control, passion must be put in its box. It is not the job of the actor playing Juliet to cry, her job is to invite the audience do so.

Since becoming an independent producer/director, most of the projects I have taken on were simply because the subject and the story interested me deeply. Hence I became passionate about placing on screen what I feel are, for me, the right results. Another director will undoubtedly present the same story differently. What we both seek is, for each of us, the 'most effective right' way to make the audience respond to 'the texture of life', the quintessential subject of documentary film whether for television or cinema.

I detest the term 'documentarist'. When permitted, I tell stories, stories that I hope will reveal, reflect and resonate. We are a country of renowned story tellers, on the page, stage, on screen. Now it would seem, from a spate of recent fine documentaries, also on the small screen. We are a country with so many 'hidden histories' still crying to be released by the pixels in the corner. Yet why are producers so often doomed to scratch around, often in vain, like so many Willy Lomans offering wares to the boys and girls in the fortresses, the ratings merchants; heads of this and that, to whom the documentary format, apart from a few honourable exceptions, still remains by them 'more honoured in the breach than in the observance'.[7]

The Faith Factor, Skill and Chance

Five years in *Would You Believe*

JULIAN VIGNOLES

I think there are two vital ingredients when it comes to successful documentary making: instinct for what makes a story and secondly, the crucial skill of knowing how to make use of chance and opportunity. You need a plan, but you need to know when it's right to change it completely. *Would You Believe*, or *WYB* (2005–10), was well established before I arrived in the office as series producer in July 2007. I was uneasy at first, particularly about the religious side of the work (niggling atheism perhaps), but I wanted to tell stories on television as I had done on RTÉ radio in previous years and here was a ready-made vehicle. I had to keep the programme's reputation up, but I didn't have the burden of starting from scratch. I had the challenge of pictures and the feeling that anyone coming from radio is assumed to be 'blind'. But I ended up staying for five years.

I learned, made mistakes and of course had to take my fair share of comment about the programmes. Faith matters got a grip of me. Why I was chosen to be series producer is to do with the internal RTÉ process of assigning producers – moving 'pieces on a chessboard', as it has often been described. I had something of a track record, having worked in RTÉ since 1979. But they were placing trust in me too. Fr Dermod McCarthy, editor of Religious Programmes at the time, was my immediate boss. He gave wise counsel and encouragement in equal measure.

The first thing you have to remember when you go to work on a series like this is that you're governed by a 'three-week turnaround'. This is limiting, but it's also great discipline in your working life. You had to shoot in week one, view and plan the next show in week two; edit and do the script and voice-over in week three. And then you were back on the road. And as series producer you had to 'manage' the rest of the operation, as well as doing your shift.

So to the work. When you went out to shoot there was no room for slippage – you had to come back with a programme. And when you went into editing on a Monday, you had to finish by Friday. Team playing becomes important. The crews and editors over the years were the people who had to put up with both our good and bad decisions, our good calls and 'fudges'.

Lighting cameramen as they are termed in RTÉ, including Breffni Byrne, Kieran Slyne, Ronan Lee or Tom Curran, could readily deliver a visual angle that you mightn't even have thought of. This was how they contributed and although in some ways 'neutral observers' with no official editorial role, I always felt they were our sternest and most useful critics. One could tell by their reaction on a shoot if the story was working. There would be a hand gesture or a whisper in your ear, or a silence at the meal break that could cause a change of tack. The sound recordists, Alan Swaine, Eddie Duffy or Cormac Duffy, had a similar influence. You have to try to lead by example of course.

My first idea, to start that 1997 season, was that we'd go to Our Lady's Island near Carnsore Point for the annual Marian pilgrimage. 'We'll film the pilgrims arriving,' I said, 'the procession, the island, the wildlife . . . We'll get Liam Griffin (then manager of the Wexford hurlers) and we'll have it all done in two days.' Sure enough we did. We also got commentary from Bishop Brendan Comiskey of Ferns (his reputation in those years as yet untarnished). In editing, I had the gritty idea of cutting the procession to U2 singing 'Wake Up Dead Man', a robust song of faith, let's say, that starts with 'Jesus, Jesus help me/I'm alone in this world/And a f—d up world it is too . . .' There was narrative in this programme, a beginning, middle and end, which I liked: buses arriving in the morning . . . preparation for the mass . . . the procession itself . . . reflections as the sun set . . .

We developed some guiding principles in the team: What's the story? Where's the faith element? Are they good talkers? Is there conflict? Heated discussion could follow. 'Remember the half hour,' I always said, 'the story has to have turns – and twists if possible – to keep the viewers to the end.' If the story is over in the first five minutes, then why would people still be watching after twenty? On *WYB* we had to balance two things: we weren't there to lecture or harangue the viewer but, on the other hand, we knew we had to have some purpose and not be neutral in the face of moral dilemmas, injustice or suffering. We had, in other words, a moral standpoint. We were left of centre really, though we liked to think we weren't for labelling like that, that we were sensitive to all human dilemmas, without any ideological bias.

For us, in a way, the purpose of the series was the 'faith element' in a story. What was the religious angle, in other words? 'That's an interesting story,' we might agree, 'but where's the faith element?' And there is this dimension to most stories that involve people in conflict situations or where they have a struggle or hardship in their lives. They reflect, they turn to a higher power, they pray. . . This dimension, far from being an impediment to making a documentary, could in fact give a programme real depth. We were, of course, often accused by colleagues of dragging in the religious or moral dimension. 'You wouldn't mind that *Would You Believe* crowd,' someone on another RTÉ programme was overheard to say, 'they do the story and then get the person to walk into the church and light a candle!'

Aside from this famous faith element, however, we developed a tabloid sensibility – we weren't afraid to allow contributors to be emotional; we liked telling it straight; we didn't care too much for the analysis of commentators. One of the first things I did was to extend the list of newspapers we got in the office from just *The Irish Times* and *Irish Independent* to include *The Star* and *Daily Mirror*. We could have our intellectual conversations, we had the ambition to make our mark both morally and televisually, but the day after the show we always wanted to know the ratings as soon as they came in. We could be brutal about people we thought were 'worthy but dull'. And Gemma McCrohan used to have a potent line if it was suggested we feature a person who had been interviewed publicly many times: 'Have they an unpublished thought?'

I had my own rule-of-thumb, which I'm not sure the team members always liked: 'We're a 25-minute show,' I'd say. 'If you come back from the shoot with eight to ten tapes, that's good. [Note: each tape was of 30 minutes' duration.] Twelve tapes in the box means you're having difficulties. More than twelve tapes and you don't really know what the story is!' Sometimes the story was made effectively before the shoot, other times the critical decisions were made on the shoot, and yet other times the difference was made in the edit suite. The relationship with the editor was often a complex one. He or she was the person who was stuck in a dark room with what you'd brought in to them. Your plan – a paper edit – was their only guide. Editors could often be sceptical about how organised you really were. Sean Farrell once characterised some producers' approach when arriving into his edit suite with a box of tapes as: 'There's a programme in there. Could you find it!?'

The series at that time was twenty-eight weeks. So they weren't all gems. Some weeks you'd be caught for time and have to settle for a story that wasn't great. This was because the plans had to be made and the crew told where they were going. You knew sometimes you were working on a 'filler', but you'd try and make the best of it – maybe something would come out of the interview? On one particular week we were making a programme about a group of Dublin women who had gone back to do the Leaving Cert after they'd raised families. I think it was the 'renewal' theme that attracted us, though to say the least, it wasn't a 'hot story'. The women were studying English, had 'discovered' and liked Patrick Kavanagh, so we went to film in Inniskeen. The Kavanagh Centre guide was showing us round the famous places and we were in the cemetery at the poet's grave, with the camera and sound rolling. He began reading from the poem *In Memory Of My Father*. One of the women suddenly broke down completely. As the tape rolled on she told us she had recently lost her father and the power of the words had stirred all kinds of memories. This moment became the highlight of a comparatively mundane programme, as it said so much about the emotional power of literature.

Of course, many programmes became even more different when the team went on the road to film them, and many's a programme was 'rescued' in editing. By adding one key interview you can transform a narrative. I remember once Jerry O'Callaghan came to us with what appeared to be a readymade programme about an Irish priest, Fr Brendan Forde, who had been filmed on location in Colombia but was later kidnapped. But we knew there wasn't enough in the material Jerry had done in the jungle, such as encounters with FARC guerrillas, or with additional references to the political situation in Colombia. However, Fr Forde had a sister, Barbara, living in Dublin who was concerned about him and admired his courage and commitment to the poor. By means of a ten-minute contribution from her, which we worked into the story, the programme was transformed. Ironically, years later he appeared on *The Late Late Show* to recount how she had died after contacting MRSA in an Irish hospital.

It was a production line on *WYB*, but you could be rewarded with great audience share if you got the story right. The most frustrating thing was going to a competition like the Prix Europa in Berlin, for example, and watching or listening to your work being totally outclassed or even put down altogether by the 'film-maker' fraternity, scorning your low-budget effort. At the same time I remember programmes that stayed with me, particularly where time was not a factor for the programme maker. In one such example, I recall a reflection on life in the Lodz ghetto in Poland, where someone had 'camped' in an archive and lovingly worked with some special photographic records there, 400 colour slides found in 1987 at a second-hand bookstore in Vienna. The pictures turned out to be photographs taken by one of the Nazis who ran the slave-labour camp. The pictures were accompanied in the programme by a ghostly narration from a survivor, who recollected his experiences at the hands of this 'photographer'. Yet the mystery – the contradiction – was how happy and smiling many people in the pictures appeared. It was a meditation on the human spirit.

Billy Wilder once said he wanted to make films where hungry people would be compelled to drop their knives and forks on the table and just stare at the screen. I always liked when someone said they 'couldn't get out of the car' they were so gripped by a radio programme. Whether programmes are 'good' or 'bad' will always be debated, but the highest compliment for programme makers will always be that people felt compelled to watch or listen.

I always liked the definition of documentary as 'the creative treatment of actuality'.[1] And that's what we modestly did in our fast turnaround – and it's still being done by others. Take the story and decide how you come at it without being predictable. I remember a Finnish radio producer once holding up the poster, the Doors of Dublin, which features period front doors, saying:

'These are beautiful front doors. But the documentary maker is the person who finds the back door.' The best programmes are the ones where you put two and two together and they add up to five – the programme gets to somewhere you hadn't planned. Gemma Cohan, researcher/reporter, and Margaret Gleeson, producer, went off once to do a programme about a well-known healer. He was full of confidence about his work. People testified about how he had transformed their lives. Then he suddenly broke down when describing how he had to deal with a tragedy in his own family. It suddenly became a bigger programme.

I remember on another occasion, one of our reporters, Eileen Good, went to see the forensic scientist Dr James Donovan, the man Martin Cahill, the gang leader, had tried to kill with a car bomb. She told me how he described his injuries, his difficulty walking, the pain he suffered and the fact that he didn't believe there was a God who could be responsible for this situation. 'That's fine,' I said, but he's described much of this before on television. Then she said: 'This is the best bit – every January on the anniversary of the bomb, he and his wife go out for dinner. They call it "The Feast of the Explosion".' Now we knew we had a story. That of course became the title of the programme. It's my favourite of all those years – the scientist with a gift for dark, droll reflections. It was the programme where I tried to be 'higher class' and have the master interview-shot not seen for as long as possible into the show. There had been a tendency in this quick turnover series to have a long interview as the foundation and then 'put pictures over it'. A more elegant approach was to find people doing real things as they spoke and 'get inside their lives' more. It would make the programme less 'static'. So we managed in this case to have Jim Donovan seen in different situations for eight minutes, I think, before the 'classic' interview-shot appeared. Then again, opportunity and chance surfaced, because in this case it was a very sunny January day. As Jim did a walking shot for us along the promenade in Bray, a place he liked, Godfrey Graham cleverly caught his shadow as it 'limped' across the shingle.

Where *Would You Believe* was placed in the schedule was significant. One big lift for us came in 1998 when our transmission time was switched from a 'God slot' on Sundays to Thursday evenings at 10.15 and, to our surprise, TV critics started to write about us. The programme had been traditionally on a Sunday in the early evening. Now we'd moved into the 'secular' mainstream of the RTÉ 1 schedule. We began to be favourably compared to the more heavily resourced *True Lives* series. And we were 'raiding' stories. The feature film about the Fethard On Sea boycott of 1957, *A Love Divided*, came out in 1999, so we headed to Co. Wexford to spend a couple of days with the man at the centre of the original controversy, Seán Cloney. Local people just wouldn't talk about those events, adding to its potency of course. Seán, since deceased, was wheelchair bound, but full of vigour and defiance for the camera.

Then we took on an even darker subject, the murder of Carl and Catherine Doyle by Mark Nash in 1997 in Co. Roscommon. It was a gripping, devastating story where faith played a role in whatever healing was possible for this family, through the part played by their local priest in comforting them. As each of the central interviewees was talked to, the elements of the story presented themselves. This is where a researcher's or reporter's contact with the person and the notes they bring back from a visit or a phone call can really make a difference.

Journalistically, we didn't shy away from certain subjects. We made a programme in 1998 called *Betrayal in Ballyfermot* which challenged the Dublin Catholic archdiocese's record of dealing with the issue of the sexual abuse of children by clergy – before the major investigations that would come some years later. A local priest whom everyone admired (and 'who did a great Elvis') had just been handed a ten-year sentence. The programme was raw testimony from the parishioners, no frills.

Then there were the painstaking investigations when Mick Peelo brought his strong journalistic ability to examine the workings of Opus Dei. Another investigation by him of a mysterious cult based in Co.Wicklow triggered one of its members to park outside my house one morning, with an implicit threat, though nothing happened when the programme was transmitted. We even tried going lighter once or twice – for example, one programme called *Is the Celtic Tiger a Christian?* exploring the economic ethics of the boom.

But always there was chance; seeing an opportunity; 'making' luck. In 2002, Áine Ní Chiaráin and I were in Dalgan Park, Co. Meath, the home of the Columban Fathers, making a profile of one of their missionary veterans, Fr Aidan McGrath, who was then well over ninety. It was going all right, we had him teeing off impressively in the local golf club. He had told stories about the 1916 Rising and his imprisonment in Mao's China for his faith. Then it was lunchtime and we sat eating in the canteen with him and two other Columban priests. As the talk went on, in generally liberal terms, Fr McGrath started to make loud noises with the knife and fork, then with his cup and saucer. He was in a rage at the 'modern' priests' views. We had a story.

Sadly, only weeks later I drove through a snowfall to pay my respects to him at his funeral, so taken was I with his spirit and charm. All of us who worked on the programme over the years were often moved by the personality or the courage of people who trusted us to tell their stories, to want to have a more personal 'follow-up' – a phone call even – after the TV work was done.

Now, looking back, there are some things that still plague my mind. Why were we not more sceptical about the Bishop of Ferns' track record on dealing with sexual abuse? Were we to some extent used by the Saddam regime in Iraq in a return journey programme we did with the ex-UN man, Denis Halliday, in 2001? Should we have been more sceptical of some of the interviewees that were 'provided'? Then there was the time that Zoltan Zinn-Collis 'departed from the script' and spontaneously turned on and raged at the German crew about their country's past as we filmed in Bergen-Belsen for *Return to Belsen* – the editor persuaded me that it wasn't worth using. And I still feel guilty about offending Fr Brian D'Arcy when he felt I used, out of context, sensitive personal interview material we'd recorded from him. Tabloid instinct on my part, I suppose. Although it was a good headline piece to end the programme – we would have been mad not to include it – I don't like offending people of his courage and calibre. And I can't leave out an embarrassing moment – nodding off watching a rough cut of another producer's programme.

I remember Neil Jordan being asked once if he had a favourite film. He said he had favourite shots instead. From those *Would You Believe* years, mine would be the occasion when Tom Curran had the camera on a long shot of Helen McKendry (daughter of Jean McConville, one of the IRA's 'disappeared')[2] as she walked through Milltown Cemetery. A Belfast black taxi kept weaving moodily through the headstones behind her. It had the look of a heavily planned shot that was, actually, accidental.

Home Truths
Prime Time investigates nursing homes and Leas Cross

Máire Kearney

It was just after 7 pm, Monday 30 May 2005, when Mr Justice Frank Clarke gave his decision to the High Court. He refused an injunction sought by the proprietors of the Leas Cross nursing home, John and Georgina Aherne, and a separate injunction by the home's matron Denise Cogley, to get the programme stopped. I jumped in my car and drove down to Windmill Lane, a post-production house on Dublin's south city quays – we had just over two hours to air. I had to sign off on the final details. Once that was done we had to play out the programme to tape – in real time. All fifty-two minutes. As soon as we had the master tape, myself and researcher Seán Mac Giolla Phádraig raced to my car and headed for RTÉ (Radio Telefís Éireann). We ran from the car park to hand deliver the tape to the anxious broadcast co-ordinator Irene Kirby in TV reception at 9.20 pm. There was just over ten minutes to air.

Home Truths (2005) is one of the many investigative documentaries produced under the *Prime Time Investigates* banner since 2003. The strand is made up of three/four hour-long documentaries broadcast on consecutive weeks in November/December and May each year. It is a separate strand from the bi-weekly current affairs programme *Prime Time*, with its own slot in the TV schedule at 9.30 pm on Monday nights. The *Prime Time Investigates* strand was instigated by the then editor of Current Affairs, Noel Curran.[1] He had returned to RTÉ in 2001 after a spell in the independent sector convinced that investigative documentaries should be a priority for current affairs. Around this time there was an increase in the licence fee and Noel saw this as an opportunity to pitch for additional resources for current affairs to put in place a new investigative strand of documentaries. The choice of name was deliberate – by putting 'investigates' in the title, Curran felt it would ensure the series was grounded in investigative journalism and would not slip into social documentary.

While current affairs had been sporadically producing investigative documentaries – most notably at that time *Cardinal Secrets* (the documentary by Mary Raftery and Mick Peelo about the Catholic Church's track record on clerical sex abuse cases broadcast in October 2002) – the difference with the new strand was that it would go out as a television series of 3/4 documentaries on consecutive Monday nights. This was seen as a way of making more of an 'event' out of these major documentaries and having a greater impact with the audience. Investigative documentaries take time and money to make and it was felt that it was important to showcase them and differentiate them from the weekly current affairs shows.

The reaction within RTÉ to the setting up of the new strand was generally positive with the recognition that investigative journalism is an essential part of RTÉ's public service remit. RTÉ has always felt that investigative journalism is one of the key standards by which its current affairs output is judged by viewers. Noel Curran, with a background in investigative journalism himself, had the ambition and confidence to make the case for the strand, push for the resources and make it a reality. By the time the first series went to air in December 2003 Noel had become managing director of Television in RTÉ and David Nally had taken over as editor of Current Affairs.[2]

The strand has been hugely successful for RTÉ both in terms of audience reach and overall impact. Since its establishment the series has maintained an average audience share well above 30 per cent. The highest audience in terms of all viewers was 'Carry On Regardless' with 783,000 (a programme on NAMA and the developers involved) at the end of 2010, followed by 'On the Edge', 773,000 viewers, in December 2008 – a documentary exploring the Travelling community's way of life. The third most popular programme achieved an audience figure of 704,000 for the investigative programme entitled 'Cocaine' in December 2007. These programmes have often generated a wide public and political discourse after broadcast and have in some cases been a catalyst that began a process of political reform.

Investigative documentaries tackle contemporary stories in a journalistic fashion and invariably there are complications and controversy along the way. The very fact of doing an hour-long investigation into, say, services for the intellectually disabled or the state of nursing homes or the planning decisions made by local councillors means that the programme makers are saying that this is a national scandal. It also means that the subject/subjects are unlikely to be happy about being featured in the programmes and thus can be anything from quietly evasive to downright obstructive to the documentary makers. It puts a great onus on the team to make sure they have the facts to back up their position.

According to David Nally, former editor of Current Affairs, when stories are being evaluated for the strand many considerations are at play. Among these are that the subject matter must be big enough to be offered to the people of Ireland as a major national issue; there must be a good chance of being able to reveal something new and important; there must be enough 'life' in it to make an appealing hour of television – in reality that usually means that it must be possible to find 'real people' who are affected by whatever alleged wrong or injustice is being investigated and will talk on camera about their experiences. The ability to actually film the wrongdoing that is taking place also makes a huge difference.

Home Truths: Pre-production, January 2005

The idea for a documentary on nursing home care came about when producer Janet Traynor and reporter Adrian Lydon were making an earlier *Prime Time Investigates* on the hospital bug MRSA in 2004. During the course of their research a nurse with experience of working in nursing homes advised them it was an area that needed attention. There had also been a number of articles in newspapers highlighting concerns about standards of care in nursing homes. An independent investigation into a Killarney public nursing home five years earlier had found evidence of substandard care over a fifteen-year period and the Health Service Executive (HSE) at the time was taking legal action against a private nursing home in Dublin for alleged breaches of the regulations.

Research on the programme started in January 2005 with a provisional transmission date for mid-May. I took up the role as producer/director in early March. Even a cursory look at the situation indicated that all was not well in the Irish nursing home sector. It became obvious that the regulatory framework and inspection regime for nursing homes was not adequate and that there were serious questions about the basic standards of care being provided in some nursing homes. So the question then became how best to tell the story.

Quite early on the decision was made to try and put someone undercover in a nursing home. Undercover filming is not undertaken lightly in any circumstances and RTÉ guidelines require all secret filming to be given prior approval from the director general – in this case Cathal Goan. But this was just one of the strands of approach being pursued. We began to look for strong stories and personal testimonies that could illustrate what was happening in Irish nursing homes and met with many families who were concerned about what was happening or what had happened to relatives of theirs that had spent time in nursing homes. We also made a number of Freedom of Information requests to get copies of HSE inspection reports and records of complaints made about particular homes to the HSE. At the time this was the only way to access this type of information and one of the reforms that happened after the programme was that inspection reports became publicly available for the first time. We were also seeking to identify key interviewees who would be able to comment overall on the national picture. We made contact with the staff of an elder abuse helpline in the UK that had noticed a big increase in callers from Ireland – particularly in relation to nursing homes – and arranged to go to London to interview them about the type of calls they were getting.

Fig. 13. Leas Cross
nursing home – image
from hidden camera

In relation to the undercover filming it was decided that rather than use a reporter it would be more appropriate and responsible to put someone in who had experience working in the health care sector. We were very conscious that we were dealing with vulnerable elderly people here and at all times our priority had to be that we would react properly and correctly to any potentially risky medical situation. Two people were recruited, including Cathal Gallagher, an experienced care assistant, and a short list of nursing homes was drawn up. We also had to put a number of elements in place to make sure that patient safety was the main concern for our care assistants – for instance we had a nurse on call during their shifts so that if they were worried about something they could get prompt medical advice on how best to deal with it.

During the course of our research serious questions had arisen about how certain homes were being run. In the case of Leas Cross, at an early stage in the research we met with Dan and Mary Moore – the brother and sister of Peter McKenna who had died from septicaemia after just thirteen days at the nursing home. Peter, who had Alzheimer's disease and Down Syndrome, died in October 2000 after he was transferred to Leas Cross against the wishes of his family. Dan and Mary were horrified by what had happened to Peter at Leas Cross – when he was admitted to Beaumont hospital he was found to be severely dehydrated and his level of hygiene was poor. He died just hours later. Dan and Mary were still traumatised by Peter's death and anxious that someone should be held accountable. The case of Dorothy Black had come before Dublin city coroner's court in January 2005. She had died from septicaemia and complicating extensive bedsores after spending nine weeks in Leas Cross in 2003. Her case was reported in the national papers as well as on RTÉ news. We tried to make contact with Dorothy's daughter Clodagh but at this stage she wasn't ready to talk to us.

But Leas Cross wasn't unique. We had a number of homes on our radar and indeed had met with many more people who were raising serious questions about other nursing homes around the country. The care assistants we identified began sending their CVs to the targeted nursing homes and quickly got jobs. Cathal Gallagher began working in the Leas Cross nursing home on 18 March. One of the most important rules we had laid down was that no filming would take place until such time as a care assistant had observed concrete examples of substandard care. In the case of Leas Cross this happened very quickly and so Cathal Gallagher was given the go-ahead to start filming.

Production, March 2005

A typical *Prime Time Investigates* team consists of a producer/director, reporter, researcher, cameraman, soundman and tape editor. They report to the executive producer of *Prime Time Investigates* and the editor of Current Affairs. The production manager within current affairs has the responsibility for managing the budget and co-ordinating the production. There are usually twenty days' filming allowed and twenty days in the offline edit – although usually these periods have to be extended as production is rarely straightforward. In the case of *Home Truths* we had the extra and novel dimension of obtaining the undercover footage.

Once the decision to film in Leas Cross was made, the technical aspects of the production had to be fine tuned. We had sourced top of the range equipment from the UK using flash card technology. The small pinhead camera was sewn into the uniform and the care assistants were trained in how to use it and how to maximise best quality picture and sound. We spent hours getting our care assistants to practise using the camera and then watching back what they had filmed. Despite this, once the real filming commenced much of the early footage was unusable. The tiny camera sat awkwardly in the shirt and the angle to film was all wrong. So some material was recorded but could not be included in the film as the protagonists weren't visible in the shot. We also had some practical problems such as what to do when the shirt needed to be washed! After each shift the material had to be downloaded, viewed and logged by a researcher and the unit powered up again ready to go. It was an enormously time-consuming process but vitally important. The care assistants were also required to give a verbal debrief to one of the team after every shift and keep a detailed log of everything that happened every working day.

There is no doubt that technological advances have impacted hugely on the way current affairs programmes are made. The extraordinary reaction to *Home Truths* shows that obtaining footage like this can impact like nothing else. To be actually able to record and broadcast footage from within the nursing home and 'show' people what was going on – instead of just 'telling' them about it – was a huge leap forward. This was the first investigative documentary from RTÉ to rely so heavily on footage obtained undercover. And although some of the early material was unusable for sound and/or vision reasons we did start to get some material that we knew would shock and horrify people because it shocked and horrified us. Footage of a skeletally thin man with gaping, oozing bedsores, a care assistant taunting a vulnerable woman, staff sleeping on duty, alarm bells being ignored – images that would come to define the documentary and end up on the front pages of newspapers all across Ireland.

As our care assistant Cathal Gallagher began to gather evidence from within the home, reporter Adrian Lydon and myself began to gather more evidence from the outside. We interviewed Dan and Mary Moore about the death of their brother Peter McKenna. We also met with Clodagh and Miriam Black whose mother Dorothy had died after spending time at Leas Cross. And through them we met with the Mullins family whose mother Kitty died after spending time there in February 2004. It took a few meetings with both families before they agreed to speak on camera about what had happened. It was quite difficult for them to talk through their experiences and it was important for them to feel comfortable with us and trust us with their stories. Also for television you need to have visual material to work with as well – in this case photographs of the deceased were required and again this can be a difficult thing for families to hand over and entrust to a production team.

Post-production, April/May 2005

During the production of *Prime Time Investigates* there comes a point where you need to start editing if you're going to make air. But in this case (and many others) at the time we needed to begin the edit, the story was still emerging and we weren't sure exactly how it was going to develop. Our edit took place in Windmill Lane studios – then based in Dublin's south docklands – and began in early April with editor Guy Montgomery and a provisional transmission date of 16 May. We were only just beginning to get some footage from Leas Cross and we were also hoping to film in other nursing homes. It was felt that we would need to include more than one nursing home in order to give a national picture and we had strong testimony on tape from people about other homes. So although we started to put together some of the Leas Cross material we were still pursuing the idea of featuring at least one other home, if not more.

But as time went on the Leas Cross evidence was so strong that it was decided that it would be sufficient to show the one nursing home as a microcosm of the national picture – of how a flawed system could allow a nursing home like that continue to operate without sanction. That decision was made very late so, as a result, much of our filming happened very late in the production schedule. We had the problem of keeping our care assistant 'undercover' – so we couldn't do interviews with anyone about conditions in Leas Cross who could potentially alert the owners to what we were doing. Or we couldn't film any exteriors of the home itself. By now our original transmission date of 16 May had been put back by two weeks to allow us more time.

There was a lot of apprehension in RTÉ about the programme and the fact that it relied so heavily on the hidden-camera footage. I was of the mind that the footage spoke for itself and that we should let it run and let people make up their own minds. The programme editors David Nally and Eddie Doyle disagreed and felt that we needed to have medical 'experts' commenting on our footage given that we weren't medically qualified to do so. It was difficult to source people in Ireland willing to do this, it being such a small country – to have a doctor criticise what was going on in a HSE-funded nursing home was a lot to ask. So we ended up looking outside the jurisdiction and persuaded two doctors to travel to Dublin and give us their professional view of the footage we had obtained. They were Dr Steven Compton, consultant old age psychiatrist from the Mater hospital in Belfast, and Dr Mary Harrington, consultant in geriatric medicine, Airedale hospital in Yorkshire in England. Their contributions were devastating; the evidence visualised on the tape was extremely damning. The programme editors were absolutely right – it just shows how easy it is to get too close to a story and how important the editorial layers are.

On 18 May our care assistant left the home after spending two months there. The following day we delivered a letter to the owners indicating that we had evidence of bad practice there and requesting an interview. We got no response but at least we could now come out into the open about what we were doing and we dispatched a crew to film exteriors of the home. We also had to make contact with the families of patients that we had on tape, inform them of what we had seen, show them the footage and hope they would allow us to use it. I was extremely concerned that the families would ask us not to use the footage but this only happened in one particular case, which obviously, we honoured. One of our central characters – a painfully thin man with horrendous pressure sores – had no contact with family or any visitors at the home. He had spent much of his life on the streets before being hospitalised and transferred to Leas Cross by the HSE. There was no one to ask permission to identify him in the footage but we felt it was inappropriate to do so and pixelated his face. It became an extremely pressurised environment within RTÉ with endless meetings and viewings with our executive producer Eddie Doyle and programme editor David Nally, and RTÉ's legal team of Éamon Kennedy and Trish Whelan, to work out what we could show and make sure that absolutely everything could be backed up. A programme like this attracts intense scrutiny on grounds of accuracy and fairness and, of course, legal exposure. Each and every line of script and every image is a potential legal case and it is crucial to be totally accurate. The edit suite is where it all comes together and yet it can be the place where the most difficult decisions and toughest calls are made.

We also alerted the HSE to what we had found and requested an interview with them. The HSE was responsible for licensing and regulating the home and they also placed a great many patients there. Under the Freedom of Information Act we had found out that Leas Cross had been the subject of a series of complaints as far back as 2001 but the home had gone without sanction. The HSE finally agreed to give us an interview but only on condition that they got to see a rough cut of the programme first. This was a very unusual situation and interviewees almost never get to see programmes before air. But in this case it was decided that we needed to get the HSE's reaction to what we had found so on the Friday before the programme was due to air, three representatives from the HSE came to RTÉ to watch the unfinished programme – it was still full of black holes etc. It was a tense viewing. After they had seen it we did the interview straight away and then it was straight down to Windmill Lane to add their reaction into the piece.

The same day – just three days before transmission – we were notified that two separate applicants had applied to get the programme stopped – the owners of the nursing home and the matron of the nursing home had sought an injunction in the High Court. We were in the edit until 5 am on Saturday morning – two days before air – and spent the weekend doing the sound mix, grade and online edit as well as attending legal meetings. On the Monday of broadcast, we were all in court while the submissions were made. In the end the judge cleared the court and sat down to watch the programme himself. After viewing it he declined to give the injunction to prevent broadcast on the basis that the programme had raised important matters of public interest. And so it was broadcast that night, Monday 30 May 2005 at 9.30.

Aftermath

The reaction to the programme was swift. The following day the HSE sent in an emergency team to take control of Leas Cross nursing home. The then taoiseach Bertie Ahern stood up in the Dáil to promise an independent inspectorate for nursing homes by the following autumn. The story became front-page news for days. The home was closed down later that summer by the HSE and has been the subject of a number of reports which found that what happened at Leas Cross constituted systemic abuse.

Making this programme was a very gruelling process for all concerned – it was hard work physically and emotionally draining and we had to turn it around very quickly – not least because the people featured in the film were in extremely vulnerable positions. Five years later a new regime of standards and inspection finally came into place, which is a significant improvement. But for the families who lost loved ones in Leas Cross it is little consolation. No one has ever been held accountable for what happened there.

Conclusion

Investigative documentaries are expensive, difficult and time consuming to make, but when they are done well they can have an enormous impact. RTÉ is the only broadcasting institution in Ireland with the resources for and the commitment to these types of documentaries. Allocating the time and production resources required to make investigative documentaries and devoting an hour in the schedule for broadcast means that these stories can explore, develop and place specific themes and issues in context. The extraordinary reaction to these programmes over the years shows that even in this multi-channel multi-platform age, television still has a huge influence and can generate a wide public and political discussion.

The very best current affairs programmes force society to confront truths that are often ignored. But programmes like this are not without risk, given that the subject matter can involve criminal matters, fraudulent activity and dangerous practices. Sometimes secret filming and covert research are necessary in order to expose these. There are other risks too. The combination of high-profile programming and robust pursuit of subject matter can mean that any errors in investigative journalism may cause significant damage.

In May 2011, RTÉ broadcast a *Prime Time Investigates* entitled 'A Mission to Prey'. As part of an investigation into sexual abuse by Irish missionaries in Africa, the programme made serious, damaging and wholly untrue allegations against a Catholic priest, Fr Kevin Reynolds. RTÉ admitted that a gross wrong had been done to Fr Reynolds and paid him an undisclosed amount in damages. Subsequently, the government requested a statutory inquiry into the circumstances surrounding the programme. At the same time, RTÉ initiated a number of inquiries.

The results of these inquiries are not known at the time of writing. Nor is it evident what the longer-term impact may be on broadcast journalism of this kind in Ireland. RTÉ has publicly stated that it must be properly accountable for its errors, just as it holds others to account through its journalism. Director General Noel Curran said in an interview on RTÉ's Six One News at the time that it is important for RTÉ to offer full accountability while also ensuring that investigative journalism is sustained as a key service priority for RTÉ.

III
Documentary:
Policy and Politics

The Life of an Independent
Film-maker
Some tales from the trenches

Donald Taylor Black

It is slightly disconcerting to realise that I have been a documentary film-maker for over twenty-five years. During that time I have witnessed more changes in film production than perhaps there have been during any other equivalent period. The use of 16mm film stock was first overtaken by Beta SP tape, then digital formats, such as digibeta, and now tape is giving way to files stored on hard drives. When I began, editing was done on Steenbeck flatbed tables in cutting rooms before non-linear post-production suites took over, where software systems such as Lightworks and Avid (both first introduced in 1989) and Final Cut Pro (1999) were in use. Film cameras and film editing still exist but digital has dominated shooting and post-production for a number of years. At the same time crews have been dramatically reduced: in the 1980s a documentary crew usually consisted of six people: director, cameraman (almost always a man), assistant camera/clapper-loader, electrician, sound recordist and production assistant. Now, in the twenty-first century it is not unusual for one person to operate the camera, record sound from an onboard microphone, and direct. However, although I have shot scenes or sequences on my own, with a mini DV camera, such as *Clongowes: The Greater Glory* (2001), I have never worked in this way for a whole shoot. On my most recent film, *David Farrell: Elusive Moments* (2008), there was usually three of us: camera, sound recordist and myself.

Of course, the changes have been more than merely technological. When I produced and directed my first documentary film, *At the Cinema Palace – Liam O'Leary*, in 1983, commissioning editors had only just been invented. The previous November, Channel 4, set up as the fourth UK channel, went on air for the first time. It had been conceived as a publisher/broadcaster, with the policy of commissioning the vast majority of its programmes from independent producers. It was therefore the model for commissioning, not solely in these islands but in Europe as a whole. Channel 4 (C4), under the dynamic and progressive leadership of its first chief executive, Jeremy Isaacs, committed itself to providing an alternative to the existing channels, an agenda which derived partly from its remit requiring the provision of programming to minority groups. Michael Kustow, its first commissioning editor for the arts, has described its policy as:

> To provide a distinctive service; to innovate in form and content; to deal with interests and groups not served by commercial television, or perhaps any television; to draw programmes from a wider range of production sources than those which constituted the existing industry.[1]

At the Cinema Palace was funded by Channel 4, Bord Scannán na hÉireann /Irish Film Board, and Irish public service broadcaster, Radio Telefís Éireann (RTÉ), with small grants from the British Film Institute and the Susan Langley Trust. The subject of the documentary was Liam O'Leary (1910–92), the veteran film-maker, cinema historian and archivist. It was of great help to me that his passionate struggle to found an Irish national film archive was a cause that was supported in principle, if not in practice, by most people in Irish cultural life and beyond. In a sense, prospective funders would be supporting Liam, his reputation and his dream, rather than me as a first-time documentary producer/director. For this reason, the British Film Institute, which had employed Liam as acquisitions officer in its National Film Archive from 1953 until 1966, was favourably disposed to the project and agreed to help, making a nominal financial contribution to the budget and assisting in a number of other ways.

Fig. 14. Crew for the production of *At the Cinema Palace – Liam O'Leary*
Poolbeg Productions' documentary
l. to r. Ken Byrne (camera assistant), Toni Delany (make-up), Kieran Horgan
(sound recordist), Sean Corcoran (cinematography), Donald Taylor Black (director), Tony Byrne (electrician) and Liam O'Leary (seated)

Immediately prior to taking up his new appointment at Channel 4, Jeremy Isaacs had produced the BBC series *Ireland: A Television History* (1981), and was both well informed about Ireland and genuinely interested in the country. Consequently, he decided that his new channel should attempt to deal with Ireland, not merely in relation to contemporary politics and/or violence as the majority of the British media was doing, but in a deeper, broader and more comprehensive manner. In order to carry out this original policy, Isaacs appointed John Ranelagh, who had worked for him as chief researcher/associate producer on the series, to be commissioning editor for Ireland and Religion [*sic*].

I had been in contact with Ranelagh when I organised and programmed the Celtic Film Festival in Wexford in 1982 so I was in an easier position to telephone him a few months later to see if C4 would be interested in getting involved in *At the Cinema Palace*. To his credit, he took a risk on a new filmmaker and initially offered a pre-sale on the UK broadcast rights, with the proviso that I use an experienced executive producer. I suggested Kieran Hickey and he agreed immediately. Kieran was a perfect choice. Although his primary interest had shifted to short fiction and television drama (*Exposure*, 1978; *The Rockingham Shoot*, 1987), and his ambition was to direct feature films, he was a respected documentary maker and an informed admirer of the work of Liam O'Leary. He assured me that, despite my relative inexperience, he would not interfere but would always be available, if and when I needed his help. Kieran also advised me to employ Sean Corcoran as my cinematographer and J. Patrick Duffner as my film editor. Sean and Pat were his partners in his production company, BAC Films, and always collaborated with him on his projects. They were ideal mentors for me, as well as being excellent technicians.

The film was shot in ten days between September 1982 and May 1983 and edited intermittently during May, June and August. It was premiered at the Cork Film Festival on 23 October and screened at the London Film Festival the following month. John Ranelagh had flown over to Dublin and viewed the film just before it was completed. Afterwards he made a couple of comments, including a query about the appropriateness of a particular piece of archive footage, and, although I cannot recall definitively, I think we may have made one very small change. Similarly, Michael Algar of the Irish Film Board and Muiris Mac Conghail of RTÉ visited the cutting room on behalf of the other principal co-funders. In all three cases the atmosphere was supportive and opinions were expressed in terms of co-operation and partnership, although I suppose I was apprehensive prior to Ranelagh's visit.

Until it set up the Independent Production Unit (IPU) in 1993, RTÉ dealt with independent film-makers through a similarly light touch. Indeed I once remember dropping a film into the controller of programmes' office only a day or two before it was scheduled to be transmitted. It may not have been looked at by him, or his deputy, before it went out although it would have been seen by a programme viewer, who checked output largely to ensure that it reached the required technical standards and did not contravene the Broadcasting Act, including – in those days – Section 31, which was concerned with proscribed political organisations. The situation in Channel 4 was somewhat different. It needed to establish a *modus operandi* because it was a publisher/broadcaster from the beginning and had to invent a new way of dealing with the companies that it commissioned. Michael Kustow explains that in the early days:

> there was the question of how much a commissioning editor should allow his or her tastes and inclinations to colour decisions. Many editors . . . felt that what was wrong with British television was the imprint of television apparatchiks, a professional class with a stake in the consensus constraining the dimensions of what television might attempt. 'Non-interventionist' was a good buzz-word in the early days; it meant interfering as little as possible in the making of a programme once we had commissioned it.[2]

Unfortunately, for genuinely independent film-makers at least, the 'apparatchiks' regained control and the light touch gave way to the heavy hand. In more recent years independents have expressed concern that broadcasters in general appear to be showing more favour to more malleable 'providers'. Naturally these 'providers' are sensitive to the dangers of 'biting the hand that feeds them'. They tend to be the increasingly business-orientated companies, which are essentially producer-led and need regular commissions to meet the costly overheads of full-time staff and office rental. Consequently they tend to make the programmes that the broadcasters want and in the style they want, thereby sacrificing their own 'independence' as film-makers. There are also younger newcomers to the industry, who understandably wish to make a good impression in order to safeguard their future careers.

However, it might be argued that there is no such thing as a genuinely 'independent' producer, at least as far as Irish television is concerned. From the 1980s onwards, RTÉ has held a dominant position, in terms of commissioning, and it does not happen as frequently as it should that the 'semi-dependents', as Rod Stoneman has called the sector, can raise finance from an alternative broadcaster, if RTÉ rejects a proposal.[3] Nevertheless, *Ballyponza*, a project of mine that was turned down by RTÉ in 1995, was submitted to BBC Northern Ireland two years later, with Belfast subjects instead of Dublin ones, and the film was completed in 1998.

Both TG4, the public service broadcaster for Irish-language speakers, which was originally established as Teilifís na Gaeilge (TnaG) in 1996, and TV3, the first commercial channel in the Republic, which went on air two years later, have changed the situation to varying degrees, partly because their smaller size allows them to be less bureaucratic and to permit quicker decisions about programme proposals. TG4 has always been a publisher/broadcaster and continues to commission a wide range of indigenous programmes from independent producers, investing up to €20 million per annum. A major Irish documentary maker told me a couple of years ago that he no longer even submitted projects to RTÉ, sending proposals instead to TG4. However, it is not a viable alternative for all independents, as, given its Irish-language remit, many subjects are unsuitable for the channel. Its budgets are also considerably lower than those of RTÉ.

TV3, on the other hand, has always relied heavily on acquired international content, particularly from the US and ITV in the UK. However, after its majority shareholder, CanWest Global, sold its stake in TV3 to venture capital company Doughty Hanson in 2006, its policy changed and the channel began to commission more independent programmes from Irish producers. In 2007 this increased by 19 per cent and, by 2009, it invested 43 per cent more on independent production than it had done three years previously. TV3 spends approximately €3 million in the sector out of its €8 million budget for original programming, which includes news. In 2005, the Broadcasting Commission of Ireland (now the Broadcasting Authority of Ireland (BAI)) instituted the Sound and Vision Fund, which has enabled TV3 (and other broadcasters) to access extra finance, under certain conditions, according to BAI guidelines, 'in support of high-quality programmes on Irish culture, heritage and experience . . .'[4] In 2009, the scheme made available approximately €8.2 million to independent producers, of which around €1.3 million was for projects to be carried or broadcast on TV3. Although this is clearly a positive development, creative documentaries are rarely screened on the channel.

In recent years, public service broadcasters around the world have felt themselves under increasing pressure from commercial rivals, particularly powerful cable and satellite companies such as Rupert Murdoch's British Sky Broadcasting (BSkyB). Consequently, their ethos and policies have been markedly compromised. Channel 4, for example, began to move away from its commitment to minorities and instead focused on the centre of the mass market. This began not so much during the reign of Jeremy Isaac's successor, Michael Grade (1987–97) but that of Michael Jackson (1997–2001). In 1999, for example, Jackson spent £100 million to reacquire the rights to the US drama series *ER*, in a joint deal which also included the situation comedy *Friends*, for which Channel 4 had lost its first-run rights to Sky 1 in 1996. Both programmes were made by Warner Bros. Television for NBC. Original homegrown drama suffered, which was no accident. When Jackson resigned in 2001, he moved to New York to become president and chief executive of USA Entertainment Company, working for Murdoch's former right-hand man,

Barry Diller. At the time of his departure, Maggie Brown wrote in *The Guardian* that:

> His second strategy for Channel 4 was to move it away from its cultural roots – '*Basically a 1960s liberal agenda*' [his phrase – my italics] – to one which was more in tune with a less ideological world.[5]

Another part of his legacy was to commission the UK version of *Big Brother*, which remained Channel 4's signature show until it was finally announced that it would not continue after Series 11 in 2010. Andy Duncan, chief executive from 2004 until 2009, had no background in programme making; he made his reputation by building the 'I Can't Believe It's Not Butter' brand in the UK, becoming European category director for Unilever's Food and Beverage Division, before moving to the BBC as director of marketing and communications. His successor, David Abraham, came into TV management after a career in advertising, where he co-founded the influential agency St Luke's. Rod Stoneman, for ten years part of the Independent Film and Video Department at Channel 4, has written that:

> Even a cursory glance at the state of Channel 4 makes it all too clear that its original aims and aspirations were being abandoned. The station, and public service television more generally, has descended into what Saul Bellow referred to as a 'moronic inferno'.[6]

However, quality and standards in RTÉ have not declined as seriously as they have at Channel 4. When I made the four-part series about Ireland's largest prison, Mountjoy, *The Joy* (1997), RTÉ not only screened it in peak time, at 9.30 pm after the main evening news, but agreed, at my suggestion, to transmit each 45-minute film without a commercial break. The series was largely observational, without a narrator, yet achieved extremely impressive figures. The third part, *In the Female Prison*, was the most highly rated programme that week, with 877,400 viewers, the first show commissioned by the IPU, in any genre, to top the ratings. RTÉ's support for, and belief in, the project was exemplary. Its courage was clearly vindicated by the success of *The Joy* in terms of audience numbers (the highest viewership of any documentary series on RTÉ before or since) and extensive media coverage, which included not only positive reviews but an editorial in *The Irish Times* and speeches in Dáil Éireann. Nevertheless, in recent years, the national broadcaster has appeared to feel that it must compete increasingly with commercial channels, both national and international, with a consequent dilution of its public service ideals. Bob Quinn, former RTÉ producer, veteran independent film-maker and member of the RTÉ Authority from 1995 to 1999, has written:

Fig. 15. *The Joy* crew on location at Mountjoy Prison
l to r: Donald Taylor Black (Producer/Director); Veronica O'Mara
(Researcher/PA); Karl Merren (SoundRecordist);
Sean Corcoran (Cinematographer)

> The country was in a crisis of growing affluence, together with the calcu-
> lated destruction of 'moribund' ideas and particularly the erosion of its
> traditional concept of an Irish identity. RTÉ was reflecting this crisis –
> and in my opinion, willy-nilly exacerbating it – while competing with the
> Goliath of broadcasting, Rupert Murdoch, and his agents on the island.
> The trouble was that RTÉ was accepting the Murdoch rules of warfare.[7]

This fear of multi-channel competition has led commissioning editors to
intervene even more closely in the making of the programmes they have commissioned. For example, they seem to be particularly concerned about the
beginnings of programmes, nervous that if their audience is not 'grabbed'
from the first thirty seconds, they will use their remote controls to search for
alternative channels. Commissioning editors appear to underestimate how
intelligent and informed their viewers actually are and, in consequence, documentaries are increasingly treated by broadcasters as if they are primarily
'entertainment'. The negative influence of advertisers, commercial sponsors,
marketing gurus and focus groups continues to grow.

In May 2007, the Screen Directors Guild of Ireland (SDGI) compiled a
short internal report on the problems facing documentary makers here and its
editor explained that:

> The editorial role of commissioning editors was highlighted. For some their editorial involvement can be strongly interventionist and intrusive . . . It is so important to state the sense that the role and input from directors is becoming less and less important to broadcasters and when a doc is commissioned by RTÉ there is this real sense that 'they are the bosses and editorially you do it their way or else'. I haven't really felt that up until pretty recently and it seems to be getting worse. It really bothers me that they are starting to bully people into making documentaries the way the comm [sic] editor wants it – with no creative flexibility.[8]

The editor of the report was more specific:

> The 'language' or 'grammar' being enforced is increasingly homogenised (the use of V/O to 'tell everything', the obligatory use of music, sound-bites, the editorial focus on sensationalism and immediate spectator gratification; not being allowed to make a point with subtlety or to explain complex issues or realities, with ambiguity or in visually innovative ways).[9]

Nevertheless, RTÉ still regularly screens documentaries on its main channel, RTÉ 1, in prime time – between 8 pm and 11 pm – and this includes arts documentaries, such as the *Arts Lives* strand. BBC 1 (network), 'the national flagship entertainment channel', hardly ever does so and, when it does, very frequently insists on a familiar on-screen presenter, who is either a journalist or a so-called 'celebrity'. This material is 'factual programming' rather than documentary. Even BBC 2, 'the national alternative entertainment and informative channel', once the home of more imaginative and thoughtful programmes, has succumbed to this 'dumbing down' process and the majority of documentaries have been ghettoised onto the excellent, but niche, BBC 4, which, according to its own website, 'aims to offer an intelligent alternative to programmes on the mainstream TV channels'. However, it is not available on terrestrial television and consequently achieves relatively small audiences. Of course, this is self-perpetuating and allows the apparatchiks to deem serious documentaries as mere 'minority' fare. RTÉ's more enlightened policy proves this to be wrong-headed.

In 2005, An Chomhairle Ealaíon / the Arts Council and the Irish Film Board initiated Documenting the Arts, a new scheme to support documentaries about Irish art and artists, as both organisations were concerned that television appeared to be becoming less interested in the arts and culture. Selected projects received automatic funding of 50 per cent (€40,000) from the Arts Council but could obtain the remaining 50 per cent from the Film Board, conditional on the support of a broadcaster. However, the financial model of Documenting the Arts was amended because the two funding bodies were of the opinion that broadcasters in general, and RTÉ in particular, were exerting too much control over those films in which they had an interest, even though they were only contributing approximately a third of the total budget. The broadcasters tended to behave as if they themselves had solely commissioned the project and were providing 100 per cent of the funding, rather than being one of three partners. It is the Arts Council's normal policy to treat its 'clients' as being responsible for producing their work with minimal or no interference, and, similarly, although the Film Board has always viewed projects in which it has a financial interest during post-production and makes suggestions to the creative team, it does not usually insist that changes are made.

The Arts Council felt so strongly about this that, under the present version of the scheme, which was launched in 2008, without the involvement of the Film Board and under the new title Reel Art, the film-maker is not permitted to raise any additional money whatsoever, the guidelines stating that one of the assessment criteria is 'the demonstrable ability of the team to complete and deliver the project with the available funds (within a total maximum budget of €80,000)'. Although film-makers have applauded the Council's decision to change the original scheme, and are delighted that they retain all rights in their projects, some feel that it is a pity that any other source of finance (including television) is now completely excluded, even in exceptional circumstances. However, film-maker Conor Horgan is not alone when he says, on the Reel Art website that 'the Reel Art scheme has provided me with the creative freedom to make the film that I want to make'.[10]

David Farrell: Elusive Moments was transmitted by RTÉ in August 2009 as part of the multi-platform *Look of the Irish* season about Irish photography. As it was funded by the Documenting the Arts scheme and then purchased as a finished piece of work via a limited licence arrangement through Programme Acquisitions, I did not have to deal with the IPU on an editorial basis. David McKenna, executive producer Cross-Media & Arts, who works closely with the IPU on the commissioning of arts programming, was responsible for putting the *Look of the Irish* strand together and made the decision to include the film after viewing it on a DVD. It was screened at its original running time of sixty-five minutes, rather than having to be cut down to the customary 'television hour' length of fifty-two minutes, although this was probably because it was transmitted at 11.05 pm at the height of summer. The disadvantage was that RTÉ paid a small licence fee, which meant that the overall budget came to considerably less than it would have done if it had been commissioned through the IPU, with a consequently lower payment for the producer/director. Nevertheless, I was delighted at the arrangement, particularly as *David Farrell: Elusive Moments* attracted an audience of 102,000 viewers, which were, as RTÉ acknowledged to me, good figures for that time of night. And, above all, it was my film.

'An Appointment to View'
The role of RTÉ's Independent Production Unit in documentary making in Ireland

KEVIN RAFTER

Introduction

Since 1993 Radio Telefís Éireann (RTÉ), the Irish national broadcaster, has operated under a statutory obligation to allocate a minimum annual budget to independent television productions. This requirement was contained in the Broadcasting Authority (Amendment) Act 1993 although it was several years before the proposal was activated. Under the legislation RTÉ has to set aside a minimum predetermined amount of money which must be lodged to a separate 'independent television programmes account'. Since 2005 RTÉ has consistently spent more than the minimum statutory limit on independent productions. For example, in 2008 the statutory minimum spend was €32.8m whereas the station's actual expenditure on independent commissioned programming was €75m. The system is managed by RTÉ's Independent Productions Unit (IPU) – more recently branded by the station as 'RTÉ Independent Commissions' – which has formalised the commissioning process, and which in addition to its own budget has its own staff who commission programmes across a variety of genres. These commissioning editors engage with independent producers and production companies to make television programmes for all areas of the station's schedule including sport, drama, entertainment and documentary.

The relationship between RTÉ and the independent television sector has over the last half-century frequently been uneasy and has often been fraught. In its initial years, most programming transmitted on the national broadcast service was produced in-house. Indeed, as recently as 1990 one independent producer described the hostile attitude within RTÉ towards independent programme makers as 'like settled people, looking out their plate-glass windows at the travellers'.[1] While inevitable tensions remain between the commissioner and the independent programme maker there is today an acceptance that 'independent productions have become a core ingredient in RTÉ's television schedules'.[2] The expansion of independent programming on RTÉ driven by the 1993 legislation – coupled with the extent and range of these commissions – has led the national broadcaster to conclude: 'From daytime to evening peak-time, during the week and at weekends, they provide some of the most popular programmes on RTÉ and also some of the most challenging.'[3] Documentary programmes are a component of this output. In a succession of annual reports from the Independent Productions Unit, RTÉ has reiterated that 'documentary programmes have always been one of the strengths of the independent sector . . .'[4]

RTÉ is not the only commissioner in the Irish market. The Irish-language television service TG4 has established a niche with independent documentary commissions while the privately owned TV3 has – as Horgan concluded – made 'steady, if unspectacular progress' since it first broadcast in 1998.[5] Yet, even with an increased interest in independent programming in recent years TV3 has made only minor moves in the direction of commissioning independent documentary productions. The reality is that RTÉ remains – as Bob Quinn asserted in 2001 – 'the only game in town', and within that context the IPU plays a dominant role.[6]

This chapter examines the impact of the IPU with a particular focus on the 2004 to 2008 period, and with specific reference to documentary programmes. Over these years the television market in Ireland was also impacted upon by the expansion in digital services which gave viewers greater choice but also increased competition for RTÉ 1 and RTÉ 2. Nevertheless, the station has remained the dominant player in the Irish television market – even in multichannel homes in 2008 RTÉ's share of adult viewers reached 38.5 per cent. Moreover, of the fifty most watched programmes on all channels in Ireland in 2008, RTÉ claimed forty-eight of the fifty places while forty-three of these forty-eight RTÉ programmes were home produced.

During this period under discussion there were significant year-on-year increases in programming expenditure which benefited independent producers including the focus in this chapter, the makers of documentary programmes. The 2004 to 2008 period also coincided with a re-positioning and re-branding of RTÉ 2 to target a younger age profile audience (in 2004) which led to a renewed focus on independent commissions on this channel. In this environment, the station claimed home-produced programmes – both commissioned and in-house – had helped to 'make RTÉ distinctive and mark us out in a crowded audio-visual landscape'.[7] In retrospect, however, this period in the first decade of the twenty-first century may come to be seen as a golden era in terms of commissioned programming expenditure. RTÉ's total spending on all programme genres from the independent sector increased from €50.8m in 2004 to a high of €79.5m in 2007. The total involved slipped back to €75m in 2008 as the first impact of the economic recession was felt on programme commissioning budgets. In this regard, the 2004 to 2008 period provides a useful insight into the evolution of RTÉ's approach towards independent commissioning prior to the recent financial retrenchment.

Section one of this chapter focuses on the IPU and its relationship with the independent sector. The total IPU expenditure on commissioned productions in the 2004 to 2008 period is examined in section two. The independent commissioning system as it has impacted upon documentary making is discussed in section three. The analysis demonstrates the significance of RTÉ and the IPU for the independent television sector and shows how what is understood by the term 'documentary' has been redefined in recent years by not just a new editorial approach but also by heightened commercial considerations.

The IPU and the Independent Television Sector

The IPU operated a single commissioning round in each of the years from 2004 to 2008 although in each year a small number of companies were invited to submit proposals through a series of limited tenders for commissions. The IPU staff judged the specific programming that required special experience or expertise not widely available in the sector. These limited tenders generally did not cover documentary programming but applied to individual strands such as lifestyle television shows *The Afternoon Show* (Green Inc.) and *The Big Bite* (Tyrone Productions) in 2004 and *Seoige & O'Shea* (Tyrone Productions), which filled a similar daytime slot on RTÉ 1 in 2006. A rolling deadline system operated for drama commissions. RTÉ's dominance in the Irish television market, mentioned previously in terms of audience share, is also evident in Table 1 which shows the level of engagement which independent producers have with the station's commissioning system.

Table 1

RTÉ AND INDEPENDENT COMMISSIONS, 2004–2008

	2004	2005	2006	2007	2008
Companies submitting proposals	341	329	365	319	189
Proposals received	1,211	1,138	1,422	1,386	1,143
Commissions awarded	193	196	199	191	164
Hours commissioned	878	1,008	1,034	1,022	833

Source: RTÉ

While the number of independent companies submitting proposals declined significantly in 2008, in the previous years all of the main Irish production companies submitted programme ideas to RTÉ. While TG4, and to a lesser degree TV3, have engaged with independent productions, the influence of RTÉ – mentioned previously – has been acknowledged by the representative body for independent production companies. In a 2007 report Screen Producers Ireland observed that the national broadcaster 'produces and commissions the production of the vast majority of television programmes produced in Ireland'.[8] The number of companies submitting proposals, the number of proposals received by the IPU and the number of commissions awarded peaked in 2006. In the same year the number of television hours commissioned from the independent sector also peaked at 1,034 hours. The impact of a slowing economy with a decline in advertising budgets can be seen in the 2008 figures when the number of awarded commissions fell to its lowest level in the period under consideration while the number of hours of television commissioned from independent producers declined significantly.

The number of production companies represented by Screen Producers Ireland (at over 170) is estimated to have increased by 140 per cent since the late 1990s. There is, however, considerable variation in the sector particularly in terms of company size. Figures provided by the IPU show how a handful of production companies in the independent sector have come to dominate the commissioning rounds. Commissions totalling €19.7m were awarded to six independent production companies in 2004 – equating to 38 per cent of the total budget on independent commissions. In the same year a further €10m – representing 19 per cent of the total budget – was awarded to another six companies. The sums received by the six independent production companies who did most business with RTÉ in 2006 increased to €23.1m (35 per cent of the total budget) while the next six companies shared in commissions valued at €12.9m, which represented 19 per cent of the total budget.

Despite a decline in overall spending on independent productions in 2008 the value of commissions awarded to the six main companies hit €25.2m, which accounted for 39 per cent of all expenditure. A further six independent production companies received €13.6m which represented 21 per cent of total spending. Effectively in 2008 twelve companies received commissions worth €33.8m out of the total budget of €75m – representing 45 per cent of all independent commissions that year. Four years previously, however, the twelve main companies who did most business with RTÉ received 58 per cent of the overall budget, indicating that there was a greater spread in commissioning expenditure between 2004 and 2008. The dominance of this group of leading companies may reflect a degree of sectoral consolidation as 'early entrants' gained an advantage with the commissioning station based on past experience of delivering quality programming on-time and on-budget.

Expenditure on Independent Commissions

Table 2 shows the minimum amount of money which RTÉ was required to spend on independent commissioned television programmes each year from 2004 to 2008. This statutory predetermined budget – coming from the 'independent television programmes account' – was the minimum spend and covered all programme genres. Between 2004 and 2008 this minimum budget requirement increased by 19 per cent.

Table 2

MINIMUM STATUTORY SPEND ON INDEPENDENT
PRODUCTIONS, 2004–2008 (€ million)

2004	2005	2006	2007	2008
€28.6	€29.4	€30.0	€31.4	€32.8

Source: RTÉ

Despite the rise in the predetermined statutory spending level, the actual increase in total RTÉ expenditure on commissioned programmes in the 2004–8 period was 47.8 per cent. The difference between the two figures is accounted for by the fact that RTÉ consistently spent in excess of its required statutory budget on independent commissions. Table 3 provides information on the statutory and non-statutory spending on independent commissions from 2004 to 2008. It is worth noting that in addition to the commissioning money provided by RTÉ, producers of independent programmes for the station also secured funding from other sources including the Section 481 tax scheme, co-production funding and the television license fee Sound and Vision scheme operated by the Broadcasting Authority of Ireland. This 'other' funding category has not been insignificant – totalling €15.7m in 2006 and €10.4m in 2007 before reaching €20.3m in 2008 of which €12.1m was for co-productions, €5.1m Section 481 and €3.1m for Sound and Vision funding.

Table 3

TOTAL SPEND ON INDEPENDENT PRODUCTIONS,
2004–2008 (€ million)

	2004	2005	2006	2007	2008
Statutory spend on independent productions	€28.9	€29.8	€30.9	€31.8	€34.4
Additional RTÉ spend on independent productions	€21.3	€43.0	€37.3	€44.7	€37.8
Total direct spend (Statutory and non-statutory) on independent commissions	€50.2	€72.8	€68.2	€76.5	€72.2
RTÉ overhead spend on independent commissions*	€0.7	€1.8	€2.2	€2.9	€2.8
Overall total spend on independent commissions	€50.9	€74.6	€70.4	€79.4	€75.0

Source: RTÉ

* The Independent Productions Unit receives office and other administrative facilities from RTÉ for which the station calculates an annual 'organisational overhead' for commissioning activities.

The figures in Table 3 for total direct expenditure on independent com-missions – including statutory requirements and non-statutory commissions – for each year is increased slightly by the addition of the overhead charge which RTÉ attributes to the IPU for office space, consumables and technical services. This organisational overhead cost increased by 300 per cent between 2004 and 2008, a rise explained by the station as 'due in part to an increase in the level of RTÉ in-house facilities to produce commissioned programmes resulting in higher levels of overhead'.[9] Staff costs at the IPU in the same period increased from €1.1m to €1.9m.

Independent Documentary Commissions

According to RTÉ, its factual programme outputs:

> . . . capture so many aspects of Irish life – from insights into the rapidly changing modern nation to revelations about the Ireland of the recent and more distant past. These are programmes that enrich the schedules in the areas of Arts, History, Religion, Enterprise, Culture and much more.[10]

Within the factual categorisation, documentaries are seen as 'a highlight of the RTÉ schedules, and offer viewers a level of engagement and depth of viewing experience often not possible in shorter form programmes'.[11] By 2008 RTÉ saw documentaries as delivering 'major landmark series, all of which delivered high ratings as well as critical and audience acclaim'.[12] These positive sentiments towards documentary output may also have been influenced by practical considerations within RTÉ – in achieving outsourced production targets docu-mentary tends to be the genre most easily delivered by the independent sector. Broadcasters will in general trust smaller independent production companies to deliver quality documentaries which do not need the type of expertise or budgets required for current affairs, sports or large scale-entertainment shows.

The published data shows that schedule slots as well as expenditure budgets have been primarily devoted to drama, entertainment and music commissions. Table 4 shows that the hours commissioned from the independent sector on documentaries ranged from 52 in 2004 to 39.5 in 2008. The hours devoted to documentary commissions actually hit 8.1 per cent of the total of independent hours in 2005 before declining to 4.7 per cent of the total in 2008. These figures for schedule time allocated to documentary commissions, however, need to be treated with some caution. The IPU has chosen to include in the annual totals for documentary programmes the ten hours of yearly output on *Crime Call* (Coco Television Productions) while in 2008 the Ernst and Young Entrepreneur of the Year – a three-hour slot – was also included under the documentary heading. Interestingly, in a departure from previous RTÉ practice in its current affairs output in 2007, a *Prime Time* slot was awarded to the independent sector, and included in the IPU documentary category.

Table 4
INDEPENDENT COMMISSIONED PROGRAMMING, HOURS, 2004–2008

	2004	2005	2006	2007	2008
Total hours on independent commissions	878	1,008	1,034	1,022	833
Total hours on documentary programming	52	81.25	58.8	61.9	39.5
% of total commissioned hours on documentary programming	5.9%	8.1%	5.7%	6.0%	4.7%

Source: RTÉ

In an initial response to the imposition of the requirement to commission a fixed amount of programming from the independent sector, John Horgan noted that not all the IPU money was spent on 'high-quality public service programmes in the areas of arts, culture and current affairs, but spread across a whole range of programming including variety programmes, gardening and quiz shows'.[13] Certainly, within the IPU factual category documentaries have received a smaller share of commissioned expenditure when compared with programming on the other two factual headings – 'Lifestyle & Daytime' and 'Regional, Education, Religion & Other Factual'. Table 5 shows the IPU spend on documentaries from 2004 to 2008. Having received a significant jump in funding between 2004 and 2005 – from €3.6m to €6.7m – expenditure declined in each subsequent year.

Table 5
IPU SPEND ON INDEPENDENT COMMISSIONED DOCUMENTARIES, 2004–2008

	2004	2005	2006	2007	2008
Total spend on documentaries	€3.6	€6.7	€6.6	€6.3	€4.3
Documentaries as % of overall direct spend on commissioned programmes	7.2%	9.2%	9.7%	8.8%	6.0%

Source: RTÉ

By 2008 only 6 per cent of spending on independent commissioned programmes in RTÉ was allocated to documentaries – the lowest percentage share in any year since 2004. The impact of the slowing economy was already evident in the 2008 figures and, on the evidence of expenditure totals, documentary commissions face being squeezed further as the economic downturn continues. The message was clearly conveyed to independent producers of factual programmes in 2010: 'Money is tight and opportunities are limited so only the best, most compelling ideas will make it.'[14]

In the 2004 to 2008 period RTÉ generally commissioned documentary programmes in single and series formats which were frequently branded under established strands such as 'True Lives', 'Arts Lives' and 'Hidden History'. There was a deliberate strategy in RTÉ in this period to prioritise arts and history documentary programming. Documentaries with arts themes tended to focus on individuals – for example commissions in 2004 included single-hour productions on Seán O'Casey (Green Crow Productions), John McGahern (Hummingbird Productions) and Patrick Kavanagh (Loopline Films). Documentary commissions continued this trend in subsequent years with programmes on Liam Clancy (Crossing the Line), Michael Colgan (Blueprint Pictures) Louis Le Brocquy (Joyce Productions), Dónal Lunny (Hummingbird Productions), John Banville (Icebox Films), Paul Muldoon (Araby Productions), Hugh Leonard (Icebox Films), John Connolly (Tyrone Productions) and Seamus Heaney (Icebox Films).

Like arts documentaries in the 2004 to 2008 period, a significant number of history documentary commissions were focused on individual figures, particularly from the nineteenth century and early twentieth century. The list of commissions included Joe Cahill (Double Band Films), Frank Aiken (Mint Productions), Eoin O'Duffy (Double Band Films) and Seán Lemass (Double Band Films). Contemporary history also featured with a four-hour series on Charles Haughey (Mint Productions) commissioned in 2004 while in 2007 a four-part series about Bertie Ahern (Mint Productions) was given the green light.

In addition to arts and history programming, observational documentaries were a staple of the station's commissioned output from the independent sector in the 2004 to 2008 period. For example, the IPU commissioned *Return to Our Lady's* (Mint Productions), which revisited individuals featured in a related series in 2003, while in a similar human interest vein there was *Junior Doctors* (Mint Productions) and *Surgeons* (Mint Productions). The 2006 commissions included *The Hospice* (Yellow Asylum Films) described by RTÉ as 'an insightful and poignant observational series following patients of Dublin's Raheny Hospice in the last days of their lives'.[15]

The IPU has been willing to run with one-off documentary ideas and had considerable audience success with the feature-length documentary *At Home with the Clearys* (Tern) about the unusual private life of Fr Michael Cleary, a high-profile Roman Catholic priest. The increase in home-produced programming on RTÉ 2 led to a number of commissioned documentary series on the second channel including *Made in the USA* which profiled successful young Irish people in America and *In Leagues Apart* fronted by Ardal

O'Hanlon which appeared prior to the 2006 World Cup. One of the biggest reactions to any documentary in the 2004–8 period was received by *The Pope's Children* (Tyrone Productions) a three-part series fronted by economist David McWilliams – another McWilliams series followed, *Generation Game* (Tyrone Productions), described as 'provocative and pacy essays on where the Irish economy and the future of our society may be headed . . . delivered strong audiences in peak-time slots'.[16] The third McWilliams series in 2009, *Addicted to Money* (Tyrone Productions), was an Irish-Australian co-production which may indicate the type of future opportunities open to independent sector firms to exploit international audiences and funding.

Seeking out new presenter talent has become a significant objective in the commissioning process alongside an increasing preference for recognisable front-of-camera figures like O'Hanlon and McWilliams. In this vein celebrity gardener Diarmuid Gavin retraced the origins of the Irish race in *Blood of the Irish* (Crossing the Line) which 'combined history and cutting-edge genealogical science in an ambitious and hugely popular two-parter'[17] while veteran news correspondent Charlie Bird fronted a number of authored travelogues. Interestingly, having emerged as a theme in the 2004–8 period, the drive for new presenters – and the promotion of a celebrity agenda – is now openly to the fore in RTÉ's approach to documentary commissions: 'Talent and presenters are key to our strategy: brilliant communicators who can bring real knowledge, insight and passion to Irish screens. If a well-known person can lead viewers through exciting, controversial or complex territory, we want to know.'[18]

While the subject matter of independent documentary commissions has been diverse, the range of programmes discussed above points to several identifiable strands in the IPU's recent approach, including the need for high-impact factual programmes to deliver ratings and – as mentioned previously – an emphasis on celebrity on-camera talent. As a dual-funded broadcaster RTÉ has statutory obligations arising from its licence fee funding but it also acts commercially in attracting advertising and responding to the competitive threat from other stations. Like its counterparts in other markets, RTÉ no longer views a television commission in isolation. The demand for multi-platform programming and the role of marketing in a competitive marketplace has impacted on commissioning decisions.

The need for high ratings has undoubtedly motivated a populist and provocative approach to documentary making. The range of commissions has pushed the genre well beyond traditional formats. The *Future Shock* strand saw commissions for speculative programmes on the impact of a property market crash, a hike in oil prices, increasing obesity, excessive alcohol consumption and water scarcity. These populist documentary programmes were matched by other commissions that also sought to stretch the traditional view of documentary film-making. The 2008 commission *If Lynch Had Invaded* (Double Band Films) offered the audience an alternative 'what if' take on the events in Northern Ireland in 1969 while a 2006 commission, *So You Want to be Taoiseach* (Midas Productions) – described as a 'witty analysis of political ambitions' – veered into light entertainment territory. Some of this type of commissioning, however, failed to deliver, including most dramatically the 2007 commissioned *High Society* (Big Mountain Productions) which mired the station in controversy over allegations of cocaine abuse in the upper echelons across Irish society.

Nevertheless, the *High Society* debacle has not muted the commercial motivation in television commissioning in RTÉ. Audience ratings increasingly play a crucial – if not the most important – role in commissioning and scheduling. For example, when seeking commissions in 2010 for its Monday 9:30 pm peak-time slot the IPU stated: 'We need the strongest, boldest, most innovative ideas to capture audiences of 30 per cent and above in this slot',[19] while in terms of arts documentaries it stated: 'We want mandatory viewing for the core arts audience and also to attract significant numbers of viewers who might not usually think of themselves as being interested in the arts.'[20]

The IPU has also advised independent producers that it was moving away from single productions and two-parter series with a new preference for 'appointment-to-view series that will keep and grow audiences across anything from 3 to 7 weeks'.[21] This strategy has been stressed for several years as the concept of 'appointment to view' emerged as an important consideration in television commissioning, with editors prioritising the need to hook an audience and then get them coming back for more. With this approach very much in mind, the focus on individual artists, in the documentary arts format, has been formally revised with a 2010 request for proposals that are 'non-biographical, high-profile, stylishly structured, intelligent and accessible'.[22] The change in approach was influenced by *The Riordans: Tea, Taboos and Tractors* (Wildfire Films) – the highest-rating arts documentary in 2009 – which took 'a substantial look at the creation and impact of the long-running drama series, structured engagingly around *Fair City* actor Aisling O'Neill's personal relationship with the programme'.[23]

Conclusion

The independent television sector has developed enormously in recent years – and this expansion has been fuelled largely by the statutory requirement on RTÉ to source programmes externally. Whereas not so long ago independent productions were a rarity on RTÉ television, today a significant amount of programming including documentary – across the station's two channels – is sourced from the independent sector in terms of hours and money. Previously, John Horgan questioned what impact there would be on RTÉ arising from the requirement to commission a greater range of independent productions, and he asked about 'implications for editorial control'.[24] It is now clear however, that through the IPU arrangement RTÉ has lost none of its editorial control. Indeed, as the station has succeeded in outsourcing more of its programming it has cemented its dominance in the market by retaining considerable control over the programmes produced by the independent sector. The enhancement of the IPU can also be seen in the significant increase in its staffing levels in recent times with positions now including a director of programmes, a deputy director of programmes and eight individuals holding the title of commissioning editor in areas such as Factual Programmes, Drama, Daytime & Lifestyle, Regional, Entertainment, Young People's, and Irish Language, Multicultural and Education.

Few documentary makers have yet gained a foothold in the international television market. The majority of independent producers remain totally dependent upon the Irish market, and within that market they are dependent almost exclusively on RTÉ. The station's dominance in the independent sector has been assisted by the absence of other English-language commissioners in the Irish market. Until the introduction of the Sound and Vision Fund, TV3 offered few opportunities for independent producers, although in more recent times the station has increased documentary slots in its schedule. Nevertheless, with the increasing ratings-driven approaches in both RTÉ and TV3 there is undoubtedly less broadcast time in national television schedules for minority programme content or experimental subject matter. The danger with a ratings and/or profit attitude in commissioning is the production of documentaries which offer 'little insight into contemporary Irish culture' or explore aspects of Ireland that are unlikely to deliver mass audiences.[25]

The discussion in this chapter has shown that the 2004 to 2008 period was an exceptionally good one for independent productions, including the makers of documentaries – the golden era as mentioned previously. In general, RTÉ expenditure was plentiful – as seen by the figures discussed – while independent commissions were shared across the sector. Nevertheless, even in this period of largesse documentaries had to fight not just for their place on an increasingly ratings-influenced television schedule in RTÉ but also for their share of the independent productions budget.

The trend in RTÉ is away from the one-off documentary films which featured so prominently in the 2004–8 period:

> We need stand-out content, innovative formats, big TV stunts and events. We'd like more humour, more reactive & investigative programming, more renewable formats; catchy titles, compelling stories, and inventive ways of telling those stories.[26]

There is now a preference for landmark series, real-life stories, well-known presenters and celebrity on-camera talent, and in the post-2008 recessionary environment, value for money.

Cláracha Fáisnéise ar TG/Documentary Programmes on TG4

RUTH LYSAGHT and RACHEL LYSAGHT

TG4 was established in 1996 with the mandate to promote 'innovation and experimentation in broadcasting'.[1] The 2001 Broadcasting Act/Acht Craolacháin (Ireland) and its updated 2009 version do not mention the Irish language as the main aim of TG4. In section (4) (a) however, it is stated that programmes should be 'primarily in Irish'.[2] To this end, the motto *Súil eile* [another perspective] is the criterion for many of TG4's commissioned projects, with the language aspect implicitly understood.[3] '[A] sense of location and identification with place and people . . . characterise[d] TnaG from the start'.[4] Since the beginning, the channel has prided itself on offering an alternative view of Irish life. This *différence* is often, but not exclusively, linked to the use of the Irish language, another means of expression and communication.[5] Broadcasting in a minority language brings a set of particular challenges.[6] The obvious difficulties which flow from a limited size and budget, which for many small stations result in an over-dependence on imported programming and formats, have in the case of TG4 been largely overcome by resourceful commissioning from a growing independent production sector, and clever twisting of formats to suit a local audience. The small pool of skilled personnel and talent who are also fluent in Irish, not to mention the linguistic ability and attitudes of its viewers, provides an extra challenge for TG4. The station meets this by seeking more visually engaging and innovative storytelling, which will be able to hold non-fluent audiences without alienating the croíphobal [core audience]. Playing with cultural markers such as language, custom and place is a sign that the culture is alive. From a producer's point of view, it means that language barriers must be overcome by creativity and visual flair.

Popular genres on minority-language television channels include children's (creating future audiences, ensuring the young hear the language in a 'fun' context), sport (hugely popular, and largely avoids language issue), music (vibrant and meaningful link to culture, without requiring high fluency of the audience) and documentary.[7] While TG4 has recently enjoyed great success with drama productions, this innovation is most visible in documentaries.

Fig. 16. Pipes traversing the land, *The Pipe* produced by Rachel Lysaght

With documentary, there is no need to 'explain' why people are speaking in the language. They simply are. This allows documentary makers a certain freedom in subject matter and approach, which is not so readily available to those creating drama.

Whose Story?

A brief look at the TG4 schedule for the week beginning 14 June 2010 reveals a diverse range of documentary topics: the legacy of Che Guevara, Mad Sweeney and his relation to the Antrim landscape, missionary activity and Gaeltacht activism, how antibiotics work, the musical gifts of the Travelling community, the 1942 escape of a German internee disguised as a woman from Mountjoy jail and reminiscences of currach-race winners from 1955.[8] The diversity of documentary subject matter indicates the broad range of interests among TG4 viewers. With an emphasis on quality, and high production values (despite ever-dwindling budgets), the station encourages producers to think of new audiences, new formats and create a strongly branded and alternative viewing platform to that offered by other broadcasters. Jerry White's comment that the work of Gael Linn effected 'translations of a mostly English-speaking country into a series of Irish-speaking images'[9] might now be reversed, as TG4 documentary (among other genres) creates spaces in which Irish is spoken 'live', even between people who would otherwise switch to English.[10]

Fig. 17. Police Cordon, *The Pipe*

Documentary in the Irish language appears to have travelled far from its early days, where expository material, frequently with an 'authoritative' voice-over in Griersonian mode, dominated the screen.[11] Indeed, until the 1970s most of the material for cinema screening in the Irish language was of an educational nature (encouraging civic spirit, domestic safety, etc), and the same film was available in an English version. Early film in Irish was pro-duced mainly by Gael Linn, whose documentary newsreels were widely shown in cinemas under the title *Amharc Éireann*.[12] State-sponsored safety films were screened as well. In the 1950s and 1960s, the Film Institute of Ireland was funded by Roinn na Gaeltachta [Department of the Gaeltacht] to dub imported films into Irish. With the advent of Radio Telefís Éireann (RTÉ), a new platform for indigenous documentary was afforded to Irish-language film-makers. However, the potential for television to provide more 'domestic' and locally coloured work was not often explored, as the tech-nology was in the hands of the few, and the 1960 Broadcasting Act set RTÉ the task of representing a 'nation'.[13] The Irish-language television station, established some thirty-six years after RTÉ, inhabits a very different techno-logical and ideological landscape. TG4 tells a different story through imaginative commissioning and original local programming. From the beginning, the 'súil eile' was linked to the documentary genre.

Local Stories

The indigenous broadcaster works in a mediascape dominated by external images of their culture and language. Much majority film, television and literature which feature indigenous characters or a 'minority' story consists of people on the outside looking in, and we rarely see the alternative: people inside looking in, or indeed people on the inside looking out (Ó Cofaigh, 2001).[14] The strength of an alternative media service could be to convey a different epistemology through similar technology, perhaps through different visual styles and attendant critiques and evaluations. The ultimate goal is to 'transform' or identify other ways of seeing and being. Such a shift in perception – from being the object of a majority gaze to a more autonomous subject who holds the camera him- or herself – leads to changes in representation. Self-representation may be realised by the engagement of real communities in the creation and telling of documentary stories. Digital technology makes this a more realistic proposition now than even ten years ago. Máire Ní Chonláin, commissiong editor at TG4, reflects on the importance of developing young talent from Gaeltacht areas:

> ... forbairt a dhéanamh le dream óga ... cén chaoi a mbeadh siadsan in ann é a chur in iúl' [developing [ideas and skills] with the young ... how might they succeed in expressing their ideas].[15]

How is the Story Told?

However, such new voices and new forms of visual storytelling are still judged by the standards that have evolved over decades of larger-scale majority cultural programming and image-making. Media conventions derived from larger language communities impose not only a certain model of practice, but also tend to promote international formats. These models of broadcasting can influence indigenous work,[16] and over-reliance on pre-existing genres and formats is sometimes to the detriment of the indigenous culture.[17] Screen practitioners recognise the usefulness of such models, but do not want to see them become the only model. As Colm Ó Tórna puts it, the indigenous broadcaster has more to offer:

> Cláracha a thugann le fios go bhfuil 'súil eile' ar an saol atá cuid mhaith ceilte ar phobal an Bhéarla [Programmes which show a 'different perspective' on the world that is to a great extent hidden from the English-language community].[18]

Indeed, Seosamh Mac Donnacha believes that part of the purpose of TG4 is to create a space for the performance of local voices 'laistigh de théarmaí tagartha agus na slata tomhais atá acusan mar phobal' [within the reference points and measuring standards of the community themselves].[19]

In addressing local issues, programme makers enter into intimate conversation with contemporary 'cultural accents',[20] or as Barclay has it, 'talking in'.[21] Homemade documentaries focus on aspects of native life which the main broadcasters had all but ignored – old people, rural areas, local history, events of significance to those in the loop – as opposed to larger-scale vistas of national import. To some degree this microcosmic approach is a sign of the times. Distrust of grand narratives or judgement leads to a personal presentation or insight into history and geography. Without the burden to represent everything, there is more room for creativity in the making of the programme. In both subject matter and approach, minority-language television channels use their cultural lode to engage with issues in a different way. The TG4 penchant for docudrama, which has led to several highly accomplished productions (for example *The Last Storyteller/An Scealaí Deireanach?* (Asylum Films and Besom Productions, 2002)), makes a strength of the small-screen specificity of televised versions of events.

Television norms and conventions are played with and twisted into new shapes, enabling a different kind of broadcasting. Bob Quinn has been a consistently strong voice in promoting distinctive production practices (which often result in visual alterity) drawn from Irish-language culture. Writing on Quinn's documentary work, *Graceville: Na Connemaras i Minnesota* (Cinegael, 1997), Marcus Ó Conaire remarks on:

> . . . the remarkable ability of the use of indigenous language to instantly elicit and articulate cultural perspective. Native documentary film which utilises native language emphasises the ability of the native lens to empower the previously unrepresented.[22]

The Māori film-maker Barry Barclay has written a series of books and articles dealing with alternative approaches to film-making and representation, based on the fact that there is a different way of thinking: 'We can reshape our priorities; we can access the [technological] tools; we know there is more to life than the nation-going-forward.'[23] It is perhaps in this area that the most interesting possibilities lie in terms of indigenous television documentary. In rethinking approaches to production, editing, scheduling and other aspects of programme making and broadcasting, producers embark on a new relationship with the conventions of television.

Why Documentary?

By investing in the drama of real stories rather than in fictions, a broadcaster can engage the audience's sense of story on a lower budget. With a broad range of documentary stories under a single 'historical/cultural' umbrella, the broadcaster can appeal to a wide audience, and by commissioning more than one production company, the benefit is manifold. Mícheál Ó Meallaigh, commissioning director at TG4, notes that the channel actively seeks innovation by working with newcomers to the industry:

> Bíonn paisean agus fuinneamh acu don ábhar agus ní bhíonn an deis céanna ar fáil ó craoltóirí móra [They have a passion and an energy for the subject, and they do not get the same chance from the bigger broadcasters].[24]

Over thirty companies were involved in the first two commissioning rounds, before the station actually came on air, and there continues to be a strong relationship between TG4 and the independent sector. In spreading their commission investment across more than one company, the broadcaster reduces risk. With the net cast wide, a variety of perspectives appear on screen, and experimentation is encouraged. To the creative possibilities of the genre, a practical advantage is also added. Documentary is a good training ground for newcomers, being less expensive to produce than drama. Although it varies depending on format and subject matter, documentary is in general relatively quick to turn around, from proposal to commission to broadcast. Ó Meallaigh reflects on the usefulness of the documentary genre in the early days of the station, as it benefited both broadcaster and developing producer:

> Le faisnéis bhí deis le ath ghearradh agus ath ghearradh agus barr feabhais a chur ar an ábhar – rud a bhí níos deacra le drámaíocht mar go raibh tú sainithe leis an footage idir láimhe. Idir an dá linn bhí an earnáil le foghlaim na ceirde [With documentary there was the chance for recutting to improve the work – something more difficult to achieve with drama where you are restricted by whatever footage you already have. During this process, people in the industry learned their craft].[25]

As TG4 continues to operate on a limited budget, many documentaries are co-funded with other bodies. *Fiosrú* (Filmbase/TG4) and *Splanc!* (Arts Council/TG4) are two such schemes. The Broadcasting Authority of Ireland (BAI) (formerly Broadcasting Commission of Ireland (BCI)) also supports projects which have the approval of a broadcaster. The search for extra funding is also encouraged by TG4, and its 2010 guidelines specifically mention that the independent producer should think of 'co-production possibilities and plans to raise financial shortfall'.[26] International co-productions make sense when the co-producing nation is non-English speaking (i.e. would require subtitling or dubbing in any event).[27]

Documentary Themes

There are currently two major documentary slots on TG4. Single one-hour documentaries are broadcast in primetime midweek under the title *Anamnocht* [The Naked Soul, or 'Soul-Revealing']. Focusing on events rather than individuals, the slot aims to explore 'fascinating aspects of our culture, heritage, history, literature and people'.[28] The Anamnocht strand has success-fully engaged with well-known and lesser-known episodes from Irish history, from *Imeacht na nIarlaí [Flight of the Earls]* (2007), following the stories of the Wild Geese who fled to Europe in 1607, to *Na Redlegs* (2009), the story of Irish slaves sent by Cromwell to Barbados where their descendents still live in poverty. These productions, demonstrating national, cross-border and inter-national resonance, are but two examples of the calibre of independent work which has been afforded a platform on TG4.

The *Cogar* [Whisper] strand of half-hour documentaries has a more inti-mate feel.[29] The commissioning guidelines for the *Cogar* series recommend that the material be 'driven by Irish-language speakers and communities, rich in content, visuals and narrative'.[30] An example of such a story is *Goodnight Ballivor, I'll Sleep in Trim* (Hawkeye Films, 2009), where the broadcaster John Quinn returns to his native Ballivor for the first time in fifty years.

Many documentaries screened on TG4 have won critical acclaim. *Mad Dog Coll* (Gaelmedia, 1999), the story of a Donegal man turned New York gangster, was one of the first to gain such recognition (2000 Irish Film & Television Academy Award for best Irish documentary). Themes of violence and conflict have been popular.[31] TG4's Thursday night slot has run drama-documentary series such as *Marú* [Murder] (Stirling Film & TV Productions, 2006), *Mobs Meiriceá* [Mobs of America] (Abú Media, 2007) and *Striapacha* [Prostitutes] (Blinder Films, 2008), which were 'loosely based around the themes of murder, criminality and justice'.[32]

The 'mirror' of television is not a straight reflection, but rather a creative interpretation. Documentary maker Desmond Bell refers to the creative use of archive in terms of storytelling resources, rather than illustrations of a scripted argument.[33] Episodes from the past are invested with significance according to their importance to the present. Therefore, the way we see the past tells more about the present than the period in question. Our memory interacts with imagination, and the truth becomes less accessible the more it is mediated and 'explained'. Even historical documentaries are a means of understanding the present and imagining what is to come, much as a rear-view mirror enables a driver to anticipate the immediate future.

The rich and complex histories of Ireland provide material for many TG4-broadcast documentaries. In 2008, in conjunction with the Irish Film Archive, a series of older documentary films was broadcast on TG4 on Wednesday nights (now available on DVD as *Seoda*). The *Uachtarán* series (Nemeton, 2007) traced the lives of the Irish presidents, and there have been several studies of famous literary and musical figures. Another important aspect of our past shown on TG4 is social history, or the stories of people who had been overlooked by mainstream versions of history, such as the Irish-speaking migrants to Belfast city in the nineteenth century, whose story was shown in *Scéal na Fadgies* (Imagine Media, 2010). Emigration has been examined in *Butte, Montana* (TG4, 2004), through the story of the Feirtéar brothers from Corca Dhuibhne who settled in America at the turn of the last century, and *Bibeanna* (Dovinia Productions, 2007) traced social and cultural change in Ireland through the eyes of twenty-five Kerry women.[34] Together, these programmes demonstrate a breadth of vision which is only possible when drawing on multiple perspectives.

International Dimension

It is obvious from the examples above that many stories connected to Ireland involve international elements. The complex relations between television, nation and the indigenous community gives rise to broadcasting which, although figured as a national public service, actually goes beyond the nation-state. TG4 has so far managed to strike a balance between the particular and the general. The danger of *leathshúileachas* [half-eye-ism], in examining the local so intently that we ignore the wider world, is offset by the range of travel programmes in particular. This is in keeping with the deliberate policy of opening Irish up to the outside world (on its own terms). TG4 has made numerous travel programmes, where exotic places are described and wondered at 'as Gaeilge'.[35] To hear unfamiliar languages translated into Irish for the viewers' comprehension puts a new complexion on the Irish itself.

Writer, explorer and programme maker Dermot Somers stresses that people in Ireland sometimes seem to have a 'subconscious Atlantis' mentality in relation to the importance of our own culture. He argues that we need programmes which move out of the country in order to contextualise this 'embedded sense of uniqueness', reflecting that when we can look at other people 'with interest and appreciation . . . we will actually reflect ourselves'.[36] By drawing on our own linguistic and cultural heritage, we may relate to other people who are also experiencing language change, such as the Nemet in Russia, as visited by Somers' series *Turas Tréadacha* [Great Nomadic Journeys].

TG4 has gained kudos from critics for its intelligent acquisition and scheduling of foreign-language programmes, particularly documentaries. It may seem ironic that foreign-language programmes provide an identity for the station, but most non-fluent speakers mention this aspect of the schedule as the most appealing to them. Ó Coileáin attributes the 'aitheantas an-láidir [atá] ag TG4, fiú ag daoine gan fhocal Gaeilge' [very strong recognition [that] TG4 enjoys, even among people without a word of Irish] to its being inclusive, and providing interesting alternatives to other national broadcasters.[37] In some ways, then, the effect of the indigenous minority station is to bypass anglophone culture in linking native and foreign-broadcast material.

Fíorscéal [True Story] is the title for a series of foreign documentaries acquired for TG4 by acquisitions executive, Deirbhile Ní Churraighín. The reversioning of international documentaries implies a dialogue between subject matter and its new host language, which often sheds new light on both. TG4 uses a mix of techniques to solve the dilemma, such as in the French-Canadian *Fíorscéal*, where the words of the original presenter are replaced with an Irish version (spoken by Ailbhe Ó Monachain), but the original interviews play in their original language, with English subtitles.[38] This makes the viewing of an international documentary on TG4 at least a tri-lingual experience (audio Irish and another language, and visual English).

Apart from trade fair acquisitions, TG4 also receives international material from its fellow minority-language broadcasters. Initiated by Māori Television in 2008, the World Indigenous Television Broadcasters' Network creates a space in which programmes and formats may be exchanged. Elements of a shared current affairs programme *Indigenous Insight* have already been screened on the partner stations, and there are plans for documentary pro-gramme-sharing in the future (Ó Gallchóir, 2008).[39]

Conclusion

Documentary is one of TG4's greatest strengths, in terms of visual creativity, encouraging the development of local voices and providing a window for Irish audiences on international matters. It has been a fertile ground for co-funding and co-production. Documentary has enticed many non-fluent viewers to engage with the stories explored on the channel. In order to continue, there is a need to continually seek new storytellers, and to nurture those who already have the camera in their hands. TG4, more so than any other broadcaster in Ireland to date, has realised the creative potential of local knowledge linked to an international context (in terms of sources, research and production itself). Although some of the innovation has occurred on insufficient budgets, its quality and ability to speak to diverse audiences demonstrates the wealth of storytelling talent in our communities. More support should be afforded to training and developing television production skills based in the regions, and our diasporic relations could be developed in creating further internationally resonant documentaries.

Digital Impacts on
Documentary in Ireland

PAT BRERETON

Introduction

There has been a long tradition of documentary film-making in Ireland, as comprehensively outlined by Harvey O'Brien in his 2004 study.[1] Documentary helps to interpret history and promote human understanding while drama- tising and sometimes bending reality. While it is often suggested that all new media simply refashion older media,[2] being digital is not always considered a defining aesthetic norm. In any case the digital documentary format is now so wide and all-inclusive, it is difficult to define much less pin down, as I illustrate using a case study of *The Rocky Road to Dublin* (1968). The growing impor- tance of new digital media is most certainly extended by the opening out of even more possibilities for production and distribution.

Thompson and Bordwell affirm in their latest edition of *Film History* how digital technology made documentary 'independent', and also made 'avant- garde filmmaking easier and cheaper', while giving non-professionals access to creative choice previously available only to high-budget film-makers.[3] Nonetheless, the authors conclude, digital tools did not revolutionise the formal and stylistic strategies established within the avant-garde or documen- tary traditions. 'They made certain effects easier to obtain, but they did not introduce a radically new aesthetic',[4] an assertion echoed by many in the industry. Also, it is strongly suggested in the literature that new digital tech- niques 'did not overturn established principles of form and style and in general the results of digital production blended seamlessly into long-estab- lished production processes'.[5]

A key focus of discussion involves teasing out the uniqueness of new digital media and mapping its specific importance for the future, as cali- brated through well-used concepts like 'interactivity', 'hypertextuality', 'database logics', increased 'access' and manipulatability of the text, alongside more obvious notions like the 'demateriality' of new digital bytes of code and information, as attributes of developments within the documentary format. The trends that began with cinema verité in the early 1960s, towards lighter, less expensive and easier to use equipment, continued to build at an ever-accelerating rate for the subsequent decades. Essentially, image-capture technologies have changed so rapidly that even well-funded professionals must constantly be ready to adapt to new formats.[6] As a result of these changes there remains a growing need for a creative and critical dialogue with new generations of audiences and film students and their differing consumption patterns. New media modes of distribution and consumption, most notably encapsulated by the web, have greatly affected our understanding of the contemporary documentary.

New Digital Formats

The DVD format for instance was examined in a special issue of *Convergence*[7] to help focus attention upon new possibilities and opportunities for audio-visual distribution and consumption. New strategies for appreciating documentary and media generally also draw on scholarship which focuses on video games logic, together with the proliferation of new modalities of computer-mediated communications, all of which are becoming evident within more contemporary audio-visual production, calling attention to how documentaries can be re-conceived, produced, distributed and consumed.

At the other end of the spectrum, multimedia teachers frequently complain that trainee documentary film-makers simply shoot too much footage, treating the digital technology like an all-encompassing cheap and disposable storage database. Often such inexperienced student film-makers have no pre-determined mindset, framed around aesthetic coherence, from which to assist the creative process of editing large data files and collating raw digital bytes of material. Echoing Lev Manovich's assertion, 'rather than seeing reality in new ways' students often simply 'pour all of it onto a hard drive'.[8] Furthermore, within film studies some purists recall the craft nature of physically cutting strips of celluloid, before manually splicing them together as a 'more intuitive' and 'creative process' for putting a film together, as opposed to what can be considered as the limitation of computer editing, where cutting and pasting is achieved too easily at the click of a mouse, often leaving no time for internalising, much less rationalising the underlying structure. Trial and error become the only modus operandi in computer manipulation. This apparent danger, embedded within the new high-speed technology with its deep storage capacity, is reiterated by one established Irish documentary editor I talked to, Tom Burke.[9]

Burke speaks of the 'huge double-edged sword' around new digital technology and DV digital cameras, which took off in the 1990s. His major concern is around 'how you can shoot so much material and how this can endlessly preclude making definite decisions on anything'.[10] The cost of full HD broadcast cameras remains very prohibitive, as is the cost of reusable memory cards. His production company shoots on Sony memory cards, which can hold up to 16 gigabytes of material – i.e. almost a full hour of high-definition footage. Having invested in four of these cards, the crew avoids running out of analogue tape when out in the field. But the film-maker accepts such advantages can leave you less disciplined in the process, by shooting too much footage. In turn, this again 'deflects decisions and categorisation till later, which can take even more time'. Nevertheless, Burke goes on to assert that 'if you find something unplanned' – like they did for instance with a flower-seller in Meath Street – they can secure really good footage, thereby 'encouraging shooting on spec'.[11]

Burke went on to note that most contemporary documentary film-makers would not even remember a time before digital. With earlier compression and computer technology, for instance, this required real time in the studio to copy footage onto the computer, which incidentally afforded time in the post-production process to closely examine and interrogate your footage. Now with new technology, however, an hour's footage can be copied onto the computer in around seven minutes – which at first appears a great saving in time – but often militates against having physical time set aside to really see your footage at a crucial stage, as facilitated within the limitations of earlier recording technologies.

Like many others, Burke firmly believes that digital and new technology generally does not define the aesthetic; in fact, reminiscent of Brown Bag's award-winning animated series *Give up Yer Auld Sins* (2001), they have consciously adapted an older analogue-like aesthetic and format to shoot their recent documentary series on the Liberties to make it more nostalgic and authentic. Some inexperienced documentary film-makers, it is suggested, often try to use every special effect imaginable, just because it's available, which is not necessarily the best approach. 'Technology should always be at the service of storytelling and not visa versa' remains a mantra many media and film teachers and scholars would also endorse.[12]

Nevertheless, it could be argued that like much analogue-based film theorising, the new digital format demands different competencies and attributes, which need to be teased out by practitioners and appreciated and understood by scholars and students. One of the most topical of these discussions revolves around 'database logic'. As Stephen Mamber suggests, database and narrative mapping is a useful tool for dealing with complexity, ambiguity, density, and information overload. It offers possibilities for approaching and explaining ideas that would otherwise be difficult to express. It is an aid to visualising – a guide, an interface, an analysis, a critical method.[13] Such digital formats, encapsulated by DVD add-ons for example, serve as a template for expressing and capturing this form of mapping and database logic.[14]

Distribution

While retaining much-needed seed funding outlets for production, from the Irish Film Board and the Arts Council among others, documentary film-makers still tend to rely on at least the possibility of getting funding and distribution through conventional 'old fashioned' public service broadcasting providers like Radio Telefís Éireann (RTÉ). Yet critics who are not at the coal face often speak of the 'rule book' for documentary film-making being re-written or even thrown out, because of the unique advantages of new digital technology. The Center for Future Civic Media (at Massachusetts Institute of Technology) for instance suggest that 'old' investigative documentary and what could be broadly categorised as public service media is in decline, since it was not directional or polemical enough to hold an audience. While at the other end of the spectrum, one wonders if documentary-inspired e-jour-nalism and all manner of blogging is as radically proactive and participatory as some appear to imply.

There certainly remains numerous examples of technological innovations in the documentary/journalism sphere, which take time to be codified within the print/broadcasting environment, much less aided and legitimated by a coherent archiving policy. Most agree that new habits of media usage inform process, choice, creation and collaboration with one another. Large public service media organisations across the world have tried to fight back against the perceived threat to journalistic practice with new forms of 'viral transmission', using for instance Citizen Tube, launched in 2007, or adapting strategies road-tested by various NGOs, alongside advertising agencies and international environmental pressure groups like Greenpeace.

Stephen Price, in a very useful comment piece from *The Sunday Times*,[15] explains how digital distribution in cinemas could help save the Irish industry. While the European Commission believes that without some public subven-tion to convert cinemas, 'one in three cinemas throughout the continent could close'. When a film is distributed, 'each 35mm print can cost upwards of €800, and they are not reusable afterwards. Digitally, on the other hand, a film can be distributed on hard drives costing €30 each, and they can be returned and recycled after use.'[16] So it appears a no-brainer for the future of the indigenous film/documentary sector to encourage cinemas to convert to digital projec-tion, as this could certainly assist our relatively impoverished audio/visual industry. But such adaptation of new technology is pricey, costing as much as €100,000 per screen. While there are insider moves afoot to support the adop-tion of new 3D technology for cinemas to meet current demands, no cinema chain is going to spend such capital outlay without government/EU support. Price concludes his review piece: 'To keep audiences coming, cinemas need to embrace digital progress; it's a case of change or die.'[17]

Furthermore, new international strategies of distribution of mass media include selling DVDs online through websites like AlterNet, Buzzflash and, of course, YouTube and SecondLife, radically changing the face of web exhibition and distribution and even archiving audio-visual material. As I discovered at a number of recent media conferences, archivists remain fully aware of the dangers of leaving such important civic and public service broadcasting decisions and protocols to commercial outlets like YouTube and Google, who are regarded as the bêtes noires of 'serious' broadcasting, much less a useful and necessary vehicle for cultural preservation of our audio-visual heritage. Nevertheless, it has to be acknowledged that with over 24 million videos online, YouTube has become the world's default archive and a growing repository for displaying and promoting all forms of documentaries. Consequently many speakers at the 2009 MIT6 conference in Boston wondered were there lessons to be learned from the likes of Facebook, YouTube and Flickr for our next generation of archivists and by extension documentary makers and consumers, or do these simply take the form of cautionary tales of crass commercial laboratory experiments, requiring close monitoring for more mainstream media cultures?[18]

SecondLife, for instance, provides some engaging new and immersive ways of looking at and creating new protocols and templates for storytelling. Are Irish documentary film-makers, one wonders, looking to such sites to help develop new formats? I was reminded of Gloria Davenport's work on narrative – when a Media Lab was set up here in Ireland – to help analyse and create fascinating new digital worlds. Much recent academic literature and criticism gravitates around YouTube, which of course has become a very large site of participatory culture and user-generated content, populated by an eclectic range of popular cultural memories. Such a global success embodies many of the so-called 'unique selling points' of new media, around speed, interactivity and participatory culture, while appearing to break the old monopolistic, top-down media corporation model and at the same time espousing a shallow yet conventional public service broadcasting ethos.

Many theorists and critics are trying to reflect on how the media industry, using email, the web and SMS, might create opportunities for audiences to become even more active. Interactivity remains both the Holy Grail and raison d'être of new digital and documentary media. These efforts to valorise interactivity, drawing on the huge commercial success of video games, can also be explained with reference to the industry's need to sustain their position in the face of increased cross-platform competition. There remains however lots of tension in fan culture especially regarding the use of YouTube, as the new media format/platform par excellence. Many question the contextualisation of videos on the site, with many radical groups wishing to be able to control consumer usage of their documentaries and in turn frame their meaning. Of course YouTube is almost designed to be context free, as it proliferates and extends its range of often ultra-short bytes of audio-visual material for indiscriminate access and consumption, which in turn remains very appealing to new generational pleasures, alongside young documentary film-makers looking for a distribution outlet. Can more conventional media outlets, like for example RTÉ in Ireland, learn from such nascent viral branding formats and distribution outlets?

Similarly the ubiquity and proliferation of the DVD format[19] can be used to help promote the audio-visual and documentary industry in Ireland by adopting its unique attributes to brand our often disparate production pipeline and more effectively increase our diasporic and world audience appeal. To illustrate this I will use a case study of *The Rocky Road to Dublin* (1968).

The Rocky Road to Dublin

As a newly defined template, DVD markets a full panoply of add-on material, which often includes commissioned documentaries that I argue, in a paper on branding Irish film, could help to extend the media industry's interconnectivity in a small audio-visual industry base like Ireland and encourage a market-branding culture. Unfortunately, there appears to be a surprisingly low level of bonus material on most Irish DVDs to date, presumably because of financial constraints and a lack of foresight in developing a national studio-like system to bolster film-making into the future. A notable exception to this remains the 2006 re-mastering of the state-of-the-nation documentary *The Rocky Road to Dublin*. This seminal documentary captures an Ireland on the brink of enormous social change. Amid scenes of everyday Irish life on the streets, in the classroom, at pubs, sporting events, dance halls, and a lively discussion among Trinity College students, the journalist/director Peter Lennon blends interviews with writer Seán O'Faoláin and Conor Cruise O'Brien, theatre producer Jim Fitzgerald, and the then editor of *The Irish Times* together with world renowned film-maker John Huston.

With the assistance of the Irish Film Archive, Rod Stoneman and the Irish Film Board agreed to finance the restoration of the old documentary and the making of a companion documentary for the DVD. The reception of the film back in the late 1960s probably ensured its cult status and fully justifies the Irish Film Board's efforts and resources at restoring the original documentary and adding *The Making of Rocky Road* (director Paul Duane) to the well-produced DVD package. This extra feature draws upon much of the contentious debate around the original release, which even though despised by the Censor's Office, could not be cut since there was no sex in it. Nevertheless, while only screened for a few weeks in one Dublin cinema, it was buried in Ireland after its initial release in 1968 and was never shown on television until recently.

Reviews include Nathan Lee's piece 'Irish Independence in the 60s, with Affection and Sarcasm', from *The New York Times*, [20] which goes on to affirm how: 'Inspired by the modernism of the French New Wave and close in tone to the wry essay-films of Chris Marker, the documentary deploys a terse, sarcastic commentary over its montage of daily life and interviews.' While in an un-attributed piece from *The Irish Times*, 'The Brainwashed leading the Brainwashed' announces how:

> Brainwashed school kids admit casually that their intellect was darkened, their will weakened and their passions inclined them to evil, patriotic sportsmen confirmed that any member of their organisation, the GAA, who plays or even looks at a 'foreign' game, such as soccer or cricket, will be expelled, university students of the newish republic tell how they are not allowed to discuss politics on campus. We counted up the modern writers who had works banned in Ireland: Truman Capote, Andre Gide, Hemmingway, Orwell, Salinger, Wells, and Irish writers from Beckett to O'Casey and Shaw.[21]

However, its spectacular life grew from its original showing at the Cannes Film Festival – the last film shown before the infamous closing down of the festival that year, spurred by Godard and others, as a result of the student revolution begun in Paris. The documentary was subsequently taken to heart by the revolutionary movement in Europe and shown widely. Now, after all these years, the documentary has come full circle and remains a provocative exposé of an important period in Irish cultural history. To celebrate this fascinating story around the production/reception of one of the most famous documentaries ever made in Ireland[22] is in itself very valuable from both a cultural and historical perspective and, I would add, helps to foreground the promotion and branding of Irish documentary as a national phenomenon, which in turn assists in growing national and international audiences for such creative indigenous productions. I would also suggest that from an Irish documentary perspective, use of such add-ons can serve as a way to promote more diverse output. Consequently RTÉ, the Film Board and other funding agencies including various tourist organisations should consider the long-term future of the industry to support the production of more 'professional' bonus features as part of the process of film-making.

As I suggested in the conclusion to my piece on branding Irish cinema:

> The brand-owning corporations of Hollywood, like all multinational companies, continue to keep looking for the 'magic bullet' that will keep competition at bay and retain their brands' highly prized status; with this aim in mind, they also strive to appropriate any opposition, by embracing the avant garde alongside national cinemas of all hues. In response, 'Irish

Cinema Inc.' with her nascent brand identity must, I believe, strategise to secure its future in the global marketplace.[23]

The documentary industry and film generally, now more than ever, must use the inherent advantages of new media and digital packaging like bonus material and more streamlined distribution methods in every way it can.[24]

Concluding Remarks

In my interview with Tom Burke, he also affirmed that television continues to be a very big outlet for their work and remains encouraged by the support of the Film Board, Arts Council as well as RTÉ in funding documentaries that are high quality and creatively driven.[25]

Pavel Barter, in a piece titled 'Talking Liberties: A documentary on the Liberties of Dublin impressively captures the spirit of a community' from *The Sunday* Times,[26] makes an interesting connection between the newly re-mastered and released *Rocky Road to Dublin* and more contemporary digital work. Local communities like the Liberties are also given a voice and a sense of place through the work of Tom Burke and others, while at the same time celebrating contemporary digital documentary and its new aesthetic potentiality.

Many recent discussions by film scholars about digital cinema focus on the special effects capabilities of digitalisation, but sometimes fail to see the way in which digital cinema has rendered reality itself a special effect. With documentary so wedded to notions of the real, digital excess and special effects most particularly call to attention the very raison d'être of the format.

Pushing at the boundaries of new media studies, Nina Wakeford from the University of Surrey in a review of the discipline raises some interesting universal research questions which should also be faced up to when examining Irish documentary production alongside all forms of new media analysis:[27]

> How do we conduct research on new media in contexts that are worlds apart from the dominant (often American) models of experience, ownership and control?
>
> How can we examine the development of new technologies through current formations of gender, class, race and sexuality?
>
> How do we create new metaphors for technological experience?
>
> How do we maintain critical dialogues with the producers of new technology?

IV
Towards the Future:
Interviews with Key
Players

Díóg O'Connell
interviews
Ken Wardrop,
Director of *His & Hers* (2010)*

DO'C: You studied film at IADT [Institute of Art, Design & Technology, Dún Laoghaire] but came to this training as a mature student. Can you tell me about your early life prior to studying at IADT?

KW: I grew up in Portarlington, Co. Laois in a Church of Ireland family. From the age of twelve I was sent off to boarding school in Co. Westmeath and then to do my Leaving Cert in High School, Rathgar, Dublin. I studied Geography and Sociology at Trinity for two years and had a ball. Then I took up a place in London on the Erasmus programme. I had an even better time there. I got a part-time job in the biggest gay night club in Europe and was staying in the halls of residence. For financial reasons I dropped out of college and got a job in a post-production company. I didn't really know what the company did other than they were involved in television. I worked as a runner in the tape library for about a year without learning how to use the tape machine. After this I took off travelling, came back to work for an architect friend who had won a contract for the Nike stores in London. I took an office job with him. Again, this developed into something bigger. The office grew from two people to twenty and I learned how to start up a business; it was a great training, particularly developing my organisation skills which stood to me later on in the film business. I eventually got bored with this job, had done an interior design course but didn't stick with this too long. I worked for a while in the Almeda Theatre following a drama course. I saw wonderful productions which got me back into the performances and production zones. Soon after I returned to Ireland.

It was the summer of 1999. Looking for work I dropped into FÁS and saw a poster advertising for a stage manager for *The Undertaking*, a wonderful stage production about a crowd of friends coming back to

* *His & Hers* was the highest grossing Irish film at the box office in 2010. It started out on ten prints, increasing to 14 across 35 sites, with the final box office figure reaching €330,000.

Ireland; one guy comes back to the family farm with his black boyfriend. I met great people and really enjoyed it and then applied to do a drama course at Trinity. Meanwhile I was living with a group of people and one of the women was getting a portfolio ready for IADT. I hung out with her and enjoyed what she was doing and decided to apply to IADT myself. I applied to the Film Production course. At that time, lots of people wanted to be directors but because of my experience in London I interviewed for the producer role and got it. It was the right time for me, I was twenty-six and I was passionate. This thing had come into my life and I knew I wanted to do it. I had done the background research. Going in saying I wanted to be a producer was already saying something.

DO'C: You spent four years at IADT culminating in your graduate film, *Undressing My Mother* (2004), which won lots of awards. What appealed to you about documentary as a form?

KW: I wasn't a cinéfile, I had no background in film. I wasn't a kid who messed around with a camera at twelve. I was starting quite fresh and first year was so exciting. We did lots of different types of projects all the time. We got to experiment with equipment. I always found myself drawn to telling real stories as opposed to fiction. I was favouring documentary over fiction. Two films I particularly liked at this time were *Festen* (1998) – the Dogma project – which was less about the art of film-making and more about the story, and a film by Michael Winterbottom which was a wonderful composite of four or five lives . . . it felt real . . . ordinary lives up on the big screen but still fascinating characters. I think they intrigued me but I had no possibility of doing that with the college resources – you had to use members of the class as actors, the emphasis then was on fiction. So rather than using them I preferred to go home and use my family because I understand them more – I knew them – so I did a project called *Hen* and the film got selected for broadcast on TV3 – everybody sees hens as intriguing . . .

DO'C: What aspect of your family was that about?

KW: Well it was more of a 'mocumentary'. I really constructed the story . . . it was about my niece trying to find a hen as a pet . . . it was just a lot of banter between a family. There was humour and a twist at the end . . . there was an element of the drama that was required for the task . . . I could just about scrape it in as a drama yet get away with using real people. I've played a lot with that through the years. I have never done documentary in its purest form because I have constructed all of my

Fig. 18. Image from *His & Hers*

stories but I've used real people and real words, their statements of reality. I tend to play with the visuals and stuff. I've never done a fly on the wall documentary, I've never done a doc where I've let the camera watch the people. I've insisted that we dictate what goes on in front of it but the words are real. I've never thought about it as a problem. The moment you enter a camera into anyone's life it stamps something on it so why not make it that I don't have to focus all the time. I'm drawn to those kinds of films, it kind of contradicts *Festen* and *Wonderland* (2003). I try to find my own combination of both, I'm still exploring and I'm still getting there.

DO'C: That comes across in *His & Hers*. The aesthetic is defined in terms of framing – we see people through windows, doors.

KW: Yeah, walking through corridors . . .

DO'C: It's almost like you're peeping around corners and doors and the theme of emotional relationships between men and women is framed and structured in this aesthetic. I thought that was a really nice dynamic.

KW: The intention behind this was partly due to budget. We had a certain budget – €100,000 – with that I was adamant about shooting on super 16. I wanted a filmic quality because I wanted to film for theatrical release rather than television and that was the agenda that the Irish

Film Board would have had anyway. With €100,000 and using super 16, pretty much half of it is gone straight away. So I knew it was going to be a really tough project. Having a defined aesthetic which would not involve moving a camera was more suitable to the budget. Technically it takes so much time and effort to set up different shots. I would have needed at least one other person – I would have needed a day to focus on everybody instead of half a day. I have loads of rules before making a film . . . that was really hard to adhere to . . . instinct is to move it but I said no, we're going to stick rigid, it's going to be a film framed in a particular way and it will have a very coherent and consistent visual and if we stick to it, it will be interpreted as something. I wasn't per se saying what that would be but I knew people would see it as a stylistic choice. I was in people's homes, their 'castles'. It's their worlds in a way that I just wanted to lock the door, just keep to one or two frames, my intention was to go with that. We've all seen those reality TV shows or wife swap shows where it's just running around. I wanted to show the similarity between the worlds we all live in, the spaces that might show the whole story as one as well, that the story would feel like we've watched one life. That was the intention of locking everything into these similar frames – it might appear as one whole that we've been moving about. If you look at the home painted in pastels – the wooden floors, roller blinds – there are similarities . . . my mom's home is like that.

DO'C: It is striking that the houses are so similar – and you're wondering again is this an aesthetic construct to tell a particular story – what struck me is that there is an order to the way people structure their lives. Is this the way you visualised it reflecting on the theme you're exploring . . . connections between the people that you don't see . . . putting an order on the external – but also the internal?

KW: No, I can't say that it was. What I was trying to achieve with the framing was to get the space so that we could concentrate on the story – so I decluttered. There was one lady that I didn't declutter and she stands out miles to me but I would declutter so that we could give more emphasis to the story than the voyeuristic things we would tend to do, but I think when you're looking at it we're concentrating on the story and the words. It was going to be extremely wordy. There was no breathing in the film where you would go through four or five minutes of music, there's no breathing . . . it's constant dialogue and a lot of that is nuanced and quite specific to our work. It takes a bit more concentrating, you don't get a break.

DO'C: So you're not distracted by the visual clutter?

Fig. 19. Image from *His & Hers*

KW: Yeah, the minute you tell someone you're going to film they do a clear-up of their house but we would also order things so that it seemed balanced. So perhaps maybe it comes across that their lives were balanced and that there was order in their lives. And you're right in that sense; what I did – and I feel proud of this – there was no villain, no baddie, they're all likeable characters. There's a lot of witty comments and sarcastic remarks but you know there's love threaded across the whole story and I guess for that reason I didn't want to throw it off balance . . . even though the reality behind some of these ladies was far deeper stories and far more heart-wrenching realities than what I was portraying. You have a lady whose husband walked out on her and never came back to her, she never saw him. A character who had had her child taken from her as a kid when she had been in one of the work houses, all these stories that they wanted to tell me because they needed to express themselves and they thought that's why I was interested. But I was interested in the ordinary. It was very hard to stick rigidly to that story – you'd go in and say 'ok, I'm dealing with character x today and I know that their story is going to be about their son' – it's very hard if they have two other sons they want to talk about, but I had to keep it on track.

DO'C: The approach is structured and organised – almost like a Hollywood feature film?

KW: Yes, I have a script in advance. I know that at thirty minutes the story was going to shift to the new kid and then we would go back and there would be a period where all the characters talk about their male child. And then we introduce the death of the father and then I would go back to the son's story and the son growing up as a teenager and then go back into the husband's story because the son has left the home and the father takes precedence and then the husband passes away and the son comes back so I had that whole narrative thread.

DO'C: Like the cycle of life . . .

KW: Yeah, a whole cycle – so I mapped it all out and I chose characters. When I met them I was: 'This character will talk about their son . . .'

DO'C: It must have involved a huge amount of research – getting to know the people?

KW: Yeah I committed a lot of the research to the two researchers that were involved, essentially what we did was we had castings, or open call where people came who heard about the project and then we had specific casting where we went to mother and toddler groups. We got a few mothers involved that way but the money wasn't vast. We stuck to a fifty-mile radius in Co. Offaly. I cut twelve to fifteen characters from the film, only because of the narrative. They were great characters, great little stories themselves but they didn't fit into the narrative . . . so that was phase one. Then I would see everybody in their own homes for an hour and then decide, yeah it's worth coming back or not. Four of us would descend for four hours into their lives – so I had to build trust and try to connect with them. These are country women – it wasn't that we were alien – I went in as a poor fellow from Laois as opposed to the chap that studies in Trinity or whatever so that the ladies would trust me and that whole bond was great, that was the best part. When I went back we were having the banter, having the chat, it wasn't an interview. It comes across in the film that we were chatting. I felt that people feel better if they're being themselves and they drop the television voice and they are delighted. They saw how the audience warmed to them by this approach.

DO'C: Are you reacting against the dominant reality style that exposes warts and all, the view that it's not a good story unless you're revealing something negative.

KW: It wasn't about that. It's not a reaction to the reality because I'm kind of a fan of it. If I look back on my influences early on, I remember being on holidays in Wales and we got BBC and we spent a week coming back to watch a series called *The Family* (BBC 1974). It was the very first reality TV show ever made, a working-class family that showed everything. We watched this as a family, fascinated. I found it intriguing, I loved it. It was hugely fascinating as an anthropological study of a family. Obviously now it's become something completely different with *Big Brother* and it's exploitative and manipulative – it's about getting the story. In a way I would have liked the original stuff. You don't have to show the cracks – you can suggest them – there are other ways and there's a hell of a lot of responsibility to the subjects.

What we've been talking about are some of the intentions that one might think one has. I had the story in mind and I had the Irish Film Board, 100 per cent backing. I didn't have to make an entertainment show; if it didn't work no one would ever see it. All those decisions that I made are the things that are strongest about it – the fact that I did decide that I would not have a villain, that I would try to tell a story that was positive. I didn't have any greater intentions beyond that . . . I think it would have been too contrived. I would have had too much influence on the characters. I'd go in and say 'tell me about your kids'. I was keeping a map of what had been talked about but in between that there was freedom, just talking about the kids and where they were in life, blending it like that.

DO'C: You shot this on super 16 and the budget was very tight. Is this in contrast to the reality TV approach and working on digital? You're working in a very different way – pre-arranged and more structured possibly?

KW: I'm fascinated by film. I'm fascinated by the fact that you don't see the immediate; you don't have any tangible thing at the end of the day to get sucked into. I'm also delighted to stop and not record everything because I'm editing everything; I had 100 as opposed to 1,000 tapes. I was prepared before going out . . . you do have your idea in place. I like to have more control, especially since I'm going to be the one editing . . . for me I will stick to a scene. A tape costs €3 – the tendency is to keep it rolling in case you miss something. I missed loads of things but I compensated and reacted and did something else that was inventive or different – the less lazy option. It would keep me from getting complacent about the character, knowing where there was a deviation, keeping them on track. I had seven minutes per character for an interview and three minutes of cutaways – and a minute and a half safety net. The problem was that super 16 is so noisy that the participants know automatically when the camera is rolling, which you wouldn't get with tape, you could just keep it on. You're nervous, wondering did

I get that? Or will it be exposed? Did I hit the pause? Was the light on? Was it in focus? All these things are crossing your mind. You're stressed about other things on the day, you spend so much more energy than you would if you were on tape, you're trying to be in top form for the interviewees but you're trying to negotiate all other elements.

DO'C: So the payoff is that you're not going through hundreds of tapes.

KW: Yes. Because I'm editing it myself I don't really like to define the story in the edit, I like to have some idea where it's going. Because I have a particular rhythm and style to my edit, I'd be thinking as I'm shooting what I'm going to be editing as opposed to some television projects where you go out and shoot and create the style thereafter. I'd be locked in my style and rhythm. I'd pause after a silence to get a bit of space. However, it didn't always work because these ladies like to talk, but you'd get a buzz when there's a great line said. However, I have to say it is not something I would choose to do again. *His & Hers* is just a specific style of film that allows that. I don't think I would get away with that too often.

DO'C: Is it a film of celebration?

KW: Oh, very much so. I think it's amusing and a celebration of something that may have been undervalued. People see it as a celebration of women and motherhood, even though all these women are working, they're business women, teachers. It is layered with all sorts of characters but at the heart is the mother and the power that they have and the fact that I think it comes across that they rule the roost and the theme of it is very much embedded. When my father passed away I realised that he may have worn the trousers and been the breadwinner but my mother was the emotional backbone and kept us together and my father would have fallen to pieces if my mom had passed away even though I always thought it would be the other way around and that's what this film, for me, is about, that emotional strength that women have that men don't have – there's a quality and I think that comes across. That's not to downgrade women who've chosen to be business women and don't put much emphasis on it. It was the story I wanted to tell, people would look at it and say why doesn't it have a gay couple? Why doesn't it have a divorced couple? That's a different story – anyone can make that – and like anyone can make this film it's just the one I chose to make. It's a celebration of my mother's life, it's the longer form of *Undressing My Mother* because I construct the narrative from my mother's life because she lost her husband. It's a celebration of a very ordinary woman though to me she's extraordinary and she's empowered four children and given them a direction in life and that's an extraordinary feat. She's not a high court judge but why shouldn't we celebrate that?

DO'C: It's also a celebration of the men in their lives – the silent voice speaks loud and that final image (it's the only time we see a man) brings it out. Is this what the story is about?

KW: Well that's it. The image of the man at the end suggests that the male story could equally be told – well that was my intention. The story is this guy's story, or all men's story. I could never do a male story; for me it was more interesting to do the female story. Not just because I'm a gay man – I think women related to me because I was talking about men, there was a different dynamic going on. And I think a female could do really good justice to the male story. It would take a female director to get it out of a man. A man to man would be a different dynamic, the humour may not have played out if a female film-maker was doing it.

DO'C: A couple of words on the distribution – your producer said if it doesn't work no one will see it but you must want to get it out there?

KW: I don't know if you made a bad film, would you want it to be shown – and we all make duds. There's the potential that you'll make a bad film and people won't like it but I do find it difficult to justify trying to sell a bad film. I can't imagine if you're getting bad reviews across the board that you'll be out there selling your film. I've had bad reviews but the good ones will tip the scale, at least you can just ignore a bad one – they were having a bad day! It's interesting that film-makers have to do that. That's the most scary thing, that I'd have to sell a film for commercial reasons, and I suppose you do have to do that but I haven't been there yet.

Before distribution comes festivals, and the festival life of a documentary is fascinating because I didn't realise that the politics of getting your film into a Grade A festival is what it's all about. Once it gets in there it takes on a life of its own, so getting Sundance to accept it was a coup because then you knew automatically that there'd be lots of interest in terms of sales abroad. Even though we had screened in London, that was our international premiere, we had aspirations for Sundance. Because we had our short films shown there, we would be on their radar as film-makers. They are very supportive of their alumni, they would have been charting us. Then they got wind of the film, they got to see it and asked us to lock it down which meant we couldn't play it anywhere else, which was unfortunate because we would have liked to play it at the Cork Film Festival but even that was not acceptable, which is totally understandable. After the first screening we sold to Australia, New Zealand and we thought 'fantastic', but really that was it. This film has a life but it's going to be in English-speaking countries – it's just too wordy, too dialogue heavy, too nuanced for it to work beyond that. The Irish theatrical release is exciting for us, very scary because it's new terrain. We've Element Distribution doing it which is great but it's taking control out of our hands which is scary for us but there's no better team for doing it in Ireland than Element.

DO'C: So where do you go from here – what's the next project?

KW: I'm committing the awful sin of doing a fiction. I'm doing *Problem Parent* – which is a story set in the Irish midlands but I'm using a combination of actors and non-actors. There'll be casting for that, it's an ongoing project. It's quite an ordinary tale, nothing too dramatic – character studies and sticking within an area that I'm familiar with. Mothering is a theme again. In this case a lady going through the menopause – she's having an early menopause and she has a window of opportunity to get pregnant. It's about that journey and her relationship with her own mother which is at the heart of it too. It's early days but I'm fairly excited to control it even more. Fingers crossed that we get there. The financing of that will be a lot more difficult and complicated – I mean one of the things with *His & Hers* was the 100 per cent financing and the complete freedom . . . it was fantastic. At the time it was quite limiting because we had originally budgeted for €250,000. But in hindsight, that was the right budget for this project. The feature will be very different.

DO'C: Is it a big challenge in Ireland to carve out a career in the film business?

KW: Oh it's impossible without the Film Board. Please God they manage to survive – there's 6,000 people employed in this business and it would be an absolute catastrophe if something was to happen to the Film Board funding.

Carol MacKeogh
interviews
Alan Maher,
Irish Film Board

CMK: What role does the Film Board play in the production of documentary?

AM: When Simon Perry became chief executive in 2006, he wanted to define the role that the Film Board played in documentary funding because up until that point it was a little unfocused as to what that role was – we seemed to be involved in quite a lot of 52-minute documentaries for television and occasionally we would do feature length documentary for the cinema –most notably the excellent *The Revolution Will Not Be Televised* (2003) and *Southpaw* (1998). When I joined in July of 2006, Simon asked me to look after our documentary output so we had to define exactly what we were doing and 2006 was at the end of a period of time when documentaries were doing very well in the cinema – there was a rebirth of sorts thanks to film-makers like Michael Moore and Morgan Spurlock and continuing interest in Errol Morris's work.

I started to work on that and we set out our stall and we decided to support documentary for the cinema – preferably feature length. We wanted our documentaries to have a strong festival life and aspire to a theatrical release. Since then we've been very committed; we've a strong allocation in our annual budget to support documentary and we've more and more tried to refine what we're doing in terms of cinema documentary. However, we continue to work with broadcasters – we worked closely with RTÉ (Radio Telefís Éireann) on *The Yellow Bittern* (2009), a documentary about Liam Clancy, which was in cinemas in 2010 and we worked closely with TG4 on a film called *The Pipe* (2010) which premiered at the Galway Film Fleadh in 2010.

We also work regularly with international broadcasters, for example with BBC Storyville which is really the flagship strand for creative documentaries in Europe and we are working with More 4 and HBO as well as other European broadcasters.

We build these relationships with broadcasters, distributors and festival programmers so that film-makers have access to these people and we try to ensure that the documentary films which we think do have real theatrical potential can reach the right people. Helping to exploit our films is a key part of what we do and relationships are vitally important.

We fully fund documentaries as well – we put up all the money for *His & Hers* (2010) and we fully funded *Pyjama Girls* (2010), which premiered at Dublin's Stranger Than Fiction Festival and we basically fully funded *Saviours* (2008) as well, which was in cinemas a couple of years ago.

CMK: When you get proposals, what criteria would you use to judge the potential?

AM: There is a core creative team that make recommendations to the Board and the Board makes the ultimate decision. What we look for is something with cinema potential which we think could really make a mark at international festivals, and even have a theatrical release. Of course, it does come down to the subject matter as well, if it's deemed as something that has been covered an awful lot on television then that is probably not something that we would do. If it is too current affairs focused then that also probably won't work for us as television does that so much better. Our films need a long shelf-life – they might take a year to finish and then the festival run might take another year – they need to be almost timeless.

What I would aspire to do since I have been here is to build a body of work with film-makers – this is difficult because it takes time – but, for example, we would hope that the next film from Ross McDonnell and Carter Gunn who directed *Colony* (2009) would be highly anticipated. Ken Wardrop, although he's interested in fiction as well, is another director with a real voice and we recently did a film with an American director, Liz Mermin, called *Horses* (2010), and over a few films with Liz you can see a style emerging as well. This isn't just about the Film Board – festivals and broadcasters look to who the director is in the first instance. We have film-makers like Alan Gilsenan, Pat Collins and John T. Davis, of course, who have already built a substantial body of work.

CMK: So, it's as much about nurturing the documentary maker and building a body of work – a critical mass?

AM: Yeah, exactly, it is about building reputations.

CMK: You mentioned international productions and co-productions – what role does Irish identity play – are there identifiable Irish themes, or is it more a case of the Irish bringing their perspective to issues abroad?

AM: There is a danger that films can be too local, with fiction films as well, so you have to try to strike a balance. *His & Hers* is a good example of a film that has a very Irish sensibility – it's very much set in Ireland in the midlands but it's also universal – it's about women and about the men in their lives. It has worked well, very well, at international festivals.

CMK: Is there a sense in which Ken's film has hit a more universal chord?

AM: Yeah, absolutely.

CMK: But would it be marketed as an Irish film?

AM: It is important that our successful documentaries are recognised as Irish productions even if the content isn't particularly Irish because this helps other productions that would follow but using Irishness as a selling point varies from documentary to documentary. One of the films where we really tried to make the Irish angle work was with *The Yellow Bittern* which we hoped would have a life in the States but it hasn't yet been picked up by an American distributor. It really should because that would play so well to the Irish diaspora and that's one where we would push the Irish aspect but in everything you are trying to find the universal.

CMK: Looking to the future, Alan, what would you see as the main impediments to documentary production in Ireland?

AM: Distribution is a huge issue – where will the film be shown. There's still so few slots for feature-length documentary on television internationally but, in terms of theatrical release, documentaries seem to go through cycles. A few years ago people were putting up money to release films but then the tide turned and we're still at that phase where distributors get nervous and they'll only make calls at rough cut stages, when they can see something, and even then they'll wait for the festivals to bid for it. And to get into the A-list festivals you really have to generate interest and it's difficult – everyone is competing for a few slots. But having said that, if you can break into that area then you can be very successful and we've managed to do that – to make an impact, albeit a small one – in the last few years where people do start to look at Irish documentaries. With *Colony* in Toronto and *His & Hers* in Sundance, there was a real buzz. Those two films made an impact – people are talking about them, people are programming them in their documentary festivals.

   And money, of course, is a big impediment. We fully funded *His & Hers* and it was a small amount of money. We need to be always looking for partners. But hopefully we've shown that this is an area where we have a lot of talent. It seems that film-makers in Ireland are naturally gifted in the arena of documentary making – there is something about the Irish sensibility that suits documentary and all we try to do is to give people an outlet for that. Using Ken as an example . . . he's been making films for years and all we really had to do is be there to support him when he was making his feature length and give him the creative freedom to do that.

CMK: That's an interesting line to develop – do you think there's an identifiable Irish style?

AM: I think there is a sensitivity and a delicacy, a sense of stillness, almost, in some of the films. I'm thinking of Alan Gilsenan, of Pat Collins and Ken Wardrop and John T. Davis; there's a sensitivity, a duty of care. In general, there hasn't been a crassness. I'm a great admirer of Michael Moore but there's a certain style of documentary . . . it's become a little tired at this stage where the film's there to support the point you want to make and you've already made up your mind before you've made the film – there is not so much of that here.

CMK: There's less a sense of discovery?

AM: Yeah, not that we wouldn't support more polemical films but what's interesting in Ireland is how good we are at producing good directors of photography. We've won best cinematography award for Michael Lavelle and Kate McCullough on *His & Hers* at Sundance, and directors of photography like Suzie Lavelle and Ross O'Donnell, who shot *Colony*, are emerging and there is a beauty to the best films that we do. It's an area where we stand out – certainly *Colony* and *His & Hers* were complimented for how they were realised and how they were shot.

CMK: You mentioned Michael Moore – his documentaries seem to prioritise entertaining and attracting an audience, but there is a conflict there. Coming back to the criteria that you've to use when you select films to fund, presumably you've to weigh audience attraction as well as the film content and style?

AM: Yes, clearly audience response is important in deciding what gets funded, and structure, it seems to me, is key to engaging an audience. Structure is as important to feature documentary as it is to television documentary but there is a big difference between television and cinema structure – it's ensuring the audience stays interested and it's finding a cinema structure that maintains interest. It's hugely important for feature-length films . . . it's ensuring that the people feel that this is a compelling piece of work without being repetitive. It is important to entertain but I also think that when people go to cinema documentary, generally speaking they're quite a committed audience, they're quite savvy and smart and literate – they could sense if, for example, there's cheating going on or if images are juxtaposed to make an inference that can't be stated openly or to make a point that isn't real or true. And especially art house audiences – who generally go to see documentaries – are very sensitive to how visual language can be manipulated. At a rough cut stage we make a call with the film-maker – we don't force everything to be feature length if we know it isn't going to sustain it. There's no point having a dull 80-min film when it would be much stronger to have a 52-min.

CMK: Looking back, what would you consider have been key documentaries – which ones stand out and what did they contribute?

AM: *Saviours* by Ross Whitaker and Liam Nolan about an inner city boxing club, was one of the first films I was involved with at the Board and that was important in that it was the first documentary in a number of years that had a theatrical release in Ireland. It did struggle to find an audience but the reviews were very strong. Another would be *Seaview* (2008), which was by Nicky Gogan and Paul Rowley and produced by Maya Derrington . . . it was very important for us as it was selected for the Berlin Film Festival – it had a long life. *Fairytale of Kathmandu* (2008) was also important – it had a long festival life – and *Waveriders* (2008) was hugely important – a surfing documentary by Joel Conroy and produced by Margo Harkin and did really well. It was the highest-grossing Irish Film Board film at the box office in 2009 and Joel Conroy is another documentary maker that I should mention – he really has a commercial sensibility and he sees things on the big screen. *The Yellow Bittern*, *Colony*, *His & Hers* all did very well on the international documentary circuit and *Horses* was the highest-rated BBC4 Storyville ever.

There are films that I wish had got a wider distribution – the Pat Collins film on Gabriel Byrne and Cathal Black's *Learning Gravity* (2007) which were both beautiful. There's a film which we almost fully funded called *Today is Better than Two Tomorrows* (2006) by Anna Rogers which had a really nice festival life – Anna is hugely talented. There are many others but I think *Colony* winning a First Appearance award at the International Documentary Festival in Amsterdam was very important and *His & Hers* winning the award at Sundance – those films made a real impact.

CMK: What future do you see for documentary in terms of the role of the Board?

AM: I would hope that the Board maintains a strong level of support for documentaries as I feel that we have only just begun to realise the potential of non-fiction film-making for the cinema here. These films are not just performing well at international festivals but films such as *His & Hers* and *Waveriders* are finding significant audiences at home too as well as critical acclaim.